Anonymous

Gems of English Song

A collection of very choice songs, duets and quartets: with an accompaniment for

the piano-forte

Anonymous

Gems of English Song
A collection of very choice songs, duets and quartets: with an accompaniment for the piano-forte

ISBN/EAN: 9783744795968

Printed in Europe, USA, Canada, Australia, Japan

Cover: Foto ©Thomas Meinert / pixelio.de

More available books at **www.hansebooks.com**

GEMS

—OF—

English Song

A COLLECTION OF VERY CHOICE

SONGS, DUETS and QUARTETS.

WITH AN ACCOMPANIMENT FOR THE

PIANO-FORTE.

BOSTON:

Published by OLIVER DITSON & CO., 451 Washington St.

New York: CHAS. H. DITSON & CO.   Chicago: LYON & HEALY.

INDEX.

RING ON, SWEET ANGELUS!

Written by H. B. FARNIE.   Music by CH. GOUNOD.

Andante moderato. (♩ = 76.)

1. Hark! 'tis the Angelus! sweet - ly ring-ing
2. Now o'er my heart a spell, gen - tly is stealing,

O'er hill   and vale,........   Hark! now the mel - o - dy   maid - ens are singing,
For words   too deep,........   When to the wander - er,   com - eth that feel-ing,

Floats   on   the gale,......... floats on   the   gale................
He   can   but weep!........ he can   but   weep!................

On such a night in years long per - ished, I too have sung, ...
I've heard the lute in dul - cet mea - sure, Neath state-ly dome, ...

Those dear old lays, so sweet, so cherished, When life was young! When life was
But ah! its tones brought me no plea-sure, A - far from home, A - far from

young! Ah! Ring on! sweet An-ge-lus, Tho' thou art shak - ing
home! Ah!

My soul to tears, ... Voi - ces long si - lent now,

With thee are wak - ing   from   out   the   years,........ from out   the

years,   With thee   are   wak - ing from out   the   years!

Oh!   sweet An - ge - lus ring   on!   Oh!   sweet An - ge - lus ring

on!   Sweet Angelus ring on!   ring   on!

Trans. by J. C. J.

M. W. BALFE.

Moderato. Recit.

VOICE.

O wilt thou share an honored name;

PIANO.

mf

f

With all my wealth, with all my fame, Say but a word; I love thee on - ly,

f

p Adagio molto.

Il-lume my heart, so sad and lone-ly, And all I have is thine, is thine.

Adagio.

p

p

Andante cantabile. Romance.

Ah! could'st thou know the bliss of lov - ing, Could'st thou but know and test my

p

pp

faith - ful love, Ah! surely then, thou, thou would'st love me, Ah! sure! Ah! sure!

thou would'st love me, Ah! surely then, thou would'st love me, thou would'st love me, then would'st thou

love me. Take, then, my heart, Al - rea-dy

thine, Thy name there-on in gold-en line is deep engraved, deep, deep! And since my heart I give to thee, Be-

stow the like fair gift on me, be-stow the like . . . . . fair gift on me.

Exchange, O, gen - - - tle la - dy dear, Enduring pledge . . of love sincere, . . .

. . . . of love sin - cere, . . . Ah ! . . . .

Ah! could'st thou know how much I love thee! Ah! could'st thou know how much I love thee!
pp
Then, surely, then, then . . . thy love would be as - sured, as - sured,
f
dim.
as-sured to me, . . Ah! la - dy dear, ah! la - dy dear,
cres.
rit.
could'st thou but know how much I love thee!
cres.
colla parte.
ff

ONE MORNING, OH, SO EARLY.

Words by JEAN INGELOW.

Music by ALFRED SCOTT GATTY.

morning, oh, so ear - ly, my be - lov - ed, my be - lov - ed, All the

birds were sing - ing blith - ly, As if nev - er they would cease, 'Twas the

Thrush sang in the gar-den, Hear the sto-ry, hear the sto-ry,. And the Lark sang "give us glo-ry," And the Dove sang "give us peace!"......

Then I listen'd, oh, so ear-ly, My be-lov-ed, my be-lov - - - ed, To the murmur from the woodland, of the dove, my dear, the dove; When the

Night - in - gale came af - ter, "Give us fame to sweet-en du - ty," When the
leggiero.
cres.
Wren sang "give us beau - ty," She made an-swer, "give us love!" She made
cres. riten. sf sf dim.
ad lib. cres. riten. f tempo 1.
an - swer, "Give us love!" She made an-swer, "Give us love!" Fair is
colla voce. riten. len.
A - pril, fair the morn-ing, My be - lov - ed, my be - lov - ed, Now for
p

us doth Spring's bright morn-ing, Wait up - on the year's in - crease, Let my

dim.

voice be heard that ask-eth Not for fame and not for glo - ry, Give for

pp e leggiero. *cres.*

Piu lento.

all our life's dear sto - ry, Give us love, and give us peace,— Give for

p *pp Piu lento.*

rall. al fine

all our life's dear sto - ry, Give us love, and give us peace."

rall.

THE YEOMAN'S WEDDING SONG.

Words by MARIA X. HAYES.

Music by PRINCE PONIATOWSKI.

morn - - - ing, And the bride so gay in fine ar -
fill - - - ing, They must not wait, they must not . . .
- ray, For the day will be now a - dorn - - -
wait, For were we late, they'd deem the groom un - will - - -
- - - - - ing.
- - - - - ing.
con brio.
Tho' I've lit - tle wealth but sov'-reign health, . . .
The sun is high in the morn - ing sky, ... And the

And   am   only   a yeoman   free, ...   When   heart . . . .   joins
lark   o'er our   heads   doth   sing, ...   A   bri - - - dal

hand,   there's none   in   the land   Can   be   rich - er   in
song   as we   gal - lop   a - long,   Keep - ing   time   to   the

joys   than   we. Ding dong, ding   dong, we'll gal - lop   a - long,   All
bells   as   they   ring. Ding dong, &c.

fears   and   doubt - ing   scorn - ing,   Ding dong, we'll gal - lop   a - long,   All fears and doubt - ing scorn - - ing, Through the val - ley we'll

haste, for we've no time to waste, As . . this . .

Solenne. *1st time.*

is . . . . my . . . wed - ding morn - - - ing.

2nd time.

wed - ding morn - - - ing.

WHEN THE THORN IS WHITE WITH BLOSSOM.

C. M. von WEBER.

When the thorn is white with blos - som, And the foun - tain flows a - gain; Tell me, Mo - ther, must I fly him, If he seek me on the plain Or the meadow; Where the primrose first is found, And be - neath the spreading beeches Many a vio - let decks the

ground, When the thorn is white with blos - som, And the foun - tain flows . , .

. . . . . a - gain. Should I at the fall of

twi-light, Hear a - far his flute's soft lays? Mother, must I close the lat - tice, If I know for me he plays? On the wil-low when en-grav'd I find my

name, If I lin-ger long to read it, Shall I hear my Mother blame? When the

thorn is white with blossom, And the fountain flows . . . . a-gain.

Tell me, if a dew-y garland Hang be-side my summer bow'r; Twin'd with leaves of fra - grant myr - tle, And each fair - est ear - ly flow'r. Must it

wi - ther, If I know he plac'd it there? Mother, tell me, would you chide me, If I

bound it round my hair? When the thorn is white with blos - som, And the

foun - tain flows . . . . . a - gain.

DOUGLAS.

Words by Miss MULOCK.

Music by LADY J. SCOTT.

1. Could ye come back to me, Douglas! Douglas! In the old like-ness that I know, I would be so faithful, so

lov-ing Douglas, Douglas! Douglas! ten-der and true.

2. Nev-er a scorn-ful word should pain you, I'd smile as sweet as An-gels do.
4. I was not half worthy of you Douglas, Not half worthy the like of you, Now

Sweet as your smile on me shone e - ver, Douglas! Douglas! ten - der and true!
all men besides are to me like shadows, Douglas! Douglas! ten - der and true!

3. Oh! to call back the days that are not,
5. Stretch out your hand to me, Douglas! Douglas!

Mine eyes were blind-ed, Your words are few. Do you know the Truth now
Drop for - give-ness, from Heaven like dew, As I lay my heart on your

up in Heaven, Douglas! Douglas! ten - der and true.
dead heart, Douglas! Douglas! Douglas! ten - der and true.

HOUR OF SWEET REPOSE.

T. H. HOWE.

1. The light is fa - - ding
2. My life's brief spring went

down the sky, The sha - dows grow and mul - - ti - ply.... I
wast - - ed by, My sum - mer's end - - ed fruit - - less - ly,.... I

hear the thrush's ev' - ning song, But I have borne with toil and
learn'd to hun - ger, strive and wait, I found you, love, oh, hap - py

wrong, so long, so long, But I have borne with toil and wrong so long.
fate, so late, so late, I found you, love, oh, hap-py fate, so late.

Dim dreams my drowsy sen-ses drown, So dar - - ling
Now all my fields are turning brown, So dar - - ling

kiss my eyelids down, Dim dreams my drowsy senses drown, So darling, darling, kiss....my eye-lids down.
kiss my eyelids down, Now all my fields are turning brown, So darling, darling, kiss....my eye-lids down.

3

Oh! blessed sleep, oh! perfect rest,
Thus pillow'd on your faithful breast,
Nor life, nor death is wholly drear,

O, tender heart since you are here,
Sweet love my soul's sufficient crown;
Now, darling kiss my eyelids down.

"LIKE THE LARK."

Words by J. OXENFORD.　　　　　　　Music by FRANZ ABT. Op. 174. No. 2.

1. Like the Lark, would I were sing - ing Thro' the a - zure plains on
2. Like the Lark, would I were drink-ing Draughts of pur - est morning
3. Like the Lark, 'twixt earth and hea - ven Could I free - ly float a-

high, O - ver hill and val - ley bring - ing, Dreams of
air, Till on dew - y flow' - rets sink - ing, I could
long, I would ri - vet earth to hea - ven, With the

high, O - ver hill and val - ley, bringing Dreams of
air, Till on dewy flow' - rets sinking I could
long, I would rivet earth to hea - ven With the

spring   a - long the   sky, Dreams of   spring   a - long the   sky,   O - ver   hill and val - ley
bask   in fragrance rare,   I   could   bask   in fragrance rare,   Till on   dew - y flow' - rets
ma - gic of my song, With the   ma - gic of my song,   I would   ri - vet earth to

bringing
sink - ing,
hea - ven

Dreams of spring,   a - long the sky,   Dreams of
I could bask   in fragrance rare,   I could
With the ma - gic of my song,   With the

O - ver   hill and val - ley   bring-ing,
Till on   dew - y flow' - rets   sink - ing,
I would   ri - vet earth   to   hea - ven,

spring along the sky.
bask in fragrance rare.
ma - gic of my song.

ONLY.

VIRGINIA GABRIEL.

1. On - ly a face at the window,   On - ly a face, nothing more ;   Yet the look in the eyes as they
2. On - ly a smile of welcome,   On - ly a smile as I pass'd ; But that smile will still be re -
3. On - ly her love I ask for,   On - ly her love, and yet ! The sweet boon I can - not

for 3d Verse.
so I must strive to for -
dim.
f
meet mine, Still comes to me o'er and o'er, On - ly a word of greet - ing,
member'd, As long as my life shall last, On - ly a woman you tell me,
hope for, And so I must strive to for - get, On - ly a word low - ly spo - ken,
for 3d Verse.
mine for - ev - er and aye
dim.
On - ly a word, that was all; Yet all day in my heart it echoed Like the sound of an an - gel's call.
On - ly a woman! to thee; But there's naught that this mere earth containeth Half so dear as this woman to me.
On - ly a "yes," would she say; It would give the sweet face at the window, To be mine for e - ver and aye.
colla voce
1st & 2nd Verse.
3d Verse.

COME WITH ME.

Words by LOUIS C. ELSON. Music by F. CAMPANA.

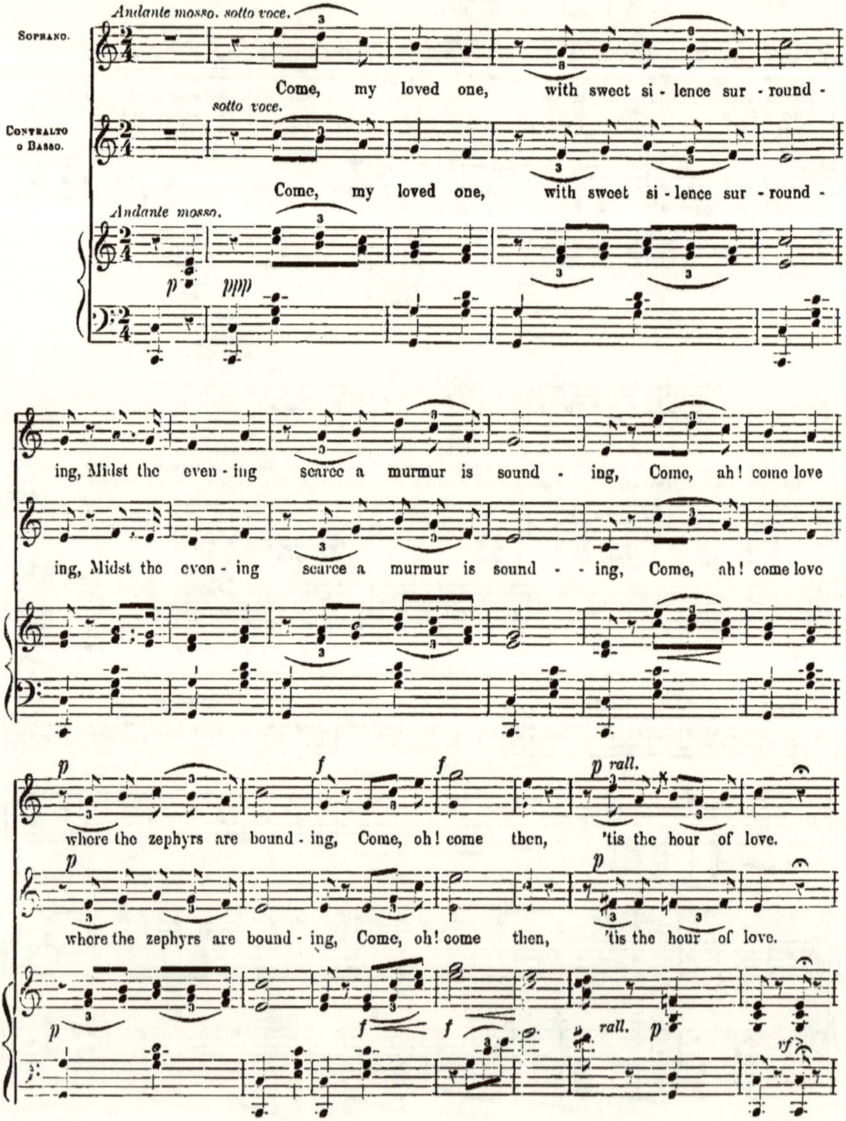

a tempo. cantabile.

Now is the calm hour of love and of

Now is the calm hour of love and of slumber,

a tempo.

slumber,

Na-ture a-round us is tran - quil - ly

Na-ture around us is tran-quil-ly gleaming.

gleaming, Waves are sleeping and ro - ses are dreaming, Soft their pet - als they si - lent - ly

Waves are sleeping and ros - es are dreaming, Soft their pet - als they si - lent - ly

34

close; Come, . . then, come . . then, ah! . . . . Come, oh! dear one,

close. Come then, come . . then, come, oh! come . . then, ah! . . . . Come, oh! dear one,

while the stars without num - ber in the a - zure of heaven are shin - ing, While the

while the stars without num - ber in the a - zure of heaven are shin - ing, While the

moonbeams with their light are en - twin - ing, Gently in - spir - ing these new songs of love.

moonbeams with their light are en - twin - ing, Gently in - spir - ing these new songs of love.

con grazia.

Now is the calm hour of love and of slum-ber, Na-ture a-round us is tran-quil-ly

'Tis the hour, 'Tis the

gleam-ing, Waves are sleep-ing, and ros - es are dreaming, Soft their pet - als they

hour, Waves are sleep-ing, and ros - es are dreaming, Soft their pet - als they

drow - si - ly close, Come then, oh, dear one, the stars without number, Midst the a - zure of

drow - si - ly close, Come, oh! dear one!

heav'n now are shin - ing, While the moon-beams with star - light en - twin-ing, Moves our

ah! come love, While the moon-beams with star - light en - twin-ing, Moves our

hearts to these new songs of love, of love, of . . .

hearts to these new songs of love, of love,

love. Moves our hearts to these new songs of love. Moves our hearts to these new songs of love.

Moves our hearts to these new songs of love. Moves our hearts to these new songs of love.

DO YOU REMEMBER?

Translated and adapted by **THEODORE T. BARKER.** Music by Sig. **CAMPANA.**

Andante sostenuto. *p con grazia.*

Dost re - call........ ....that summer night, love, When the

Dost re - call...........that summer night, love, When the

PIANO *f*

heav'ns we gazed on to-geth - er, How with pure................... e - the - real

heav'ns we gazed on to-geth - er, How with pure...... .... e - the - real
con espress.

sf

a tempo.

light,........... love, Planets gem'd the veil of blue. In its

light,........... love, Planets gem'd the veil of blue.

p

pathway, thy star resplendent, As we watch'd it, did mine pur-

partante.

In its pathway my star resplendent, As we watch'd it,

-sue........ Spoke of love,........... and then as-cend--ant, In a

did mine pur-sue. Spoke of love,........... and then as-cend--ant, In a

parlante con grazia.

flash, was lost to view, Dost recall that summer night love, when the heav'ns we watch'd to-

flash, was lost to view. Ah!..............

accel a poco.

gother,How with pure e-thereal light,love,Planets gem'd the veil of blue, Dost re-

yes! Ah! yes, I recall it,

sf

stacc. accel a poco.

- call it? ah yes, When I whis - pered of love, the

I recall it, ah........ yes, When I whis - pered of love, the

cres. *a tempo.*

plan - et Brightly flashing,while we gazed,was lost to view.

plan - et Brightly flashing,while we gazed was lost to view, In its course thy star re-

Spoke of love, and then as . cendant, In a flash was lost to

splendent, as we watch'd did mine pursue.

view. Dost recall it? ah! yes. While I

I recall it. I recall it, ah?.... yes. While I

accel a poco
cres.

con grazia.

whispered of love, the plan - et............ Brightly flashing, As we gazed, was lost to

whispered of love, the plan - et............ Brightly flashing, As we gazed, was lost to a tempo.

view. Ah!................ my own........ love, oh! dearest

view. Oh dear - est love! Ah!................. my own........ love.

a tempo.

love, my own, my dear - est. Ah!............... yes, Ah! my

my own, my dear - est, Ah!............ yes, thou'rt my own love,

rall. a piacere.

own love, yes, all my own..

yes, all my own.....................................

col canto.

DO I LOVE THEE?

J. WIEGAND. Op. 34.

Andante quasi allegretto.

PIANO.

Do I love thee? ask the bee If she loves . . . . the flow'-ry

lea, Where the ho - ney-suc - kle blows, And the fra - - grant clo - ver

grows? As she an - - swers yes or no; Dar-ling, take . . . my answer so; . . . As she an - - swers yes or no, . . . Darling, take . . my answer

so ; Do I love thee? Ask the

bird . . When her ma - - tin song is heard, If she loves . . the sky so

poco. ac - - cel - le - - ran - - do.

fair? Flee - cy cloud, . . and li - quid air? . . . As she an - - swers yes or no,   Darling, take... my answer so;... As she an - - swers yes or

no,.... Dar - ling, take.... my answer so...

calando.

pp slower. con espressione.

Do I love thee? Ask the flow - er If she loves.. the ver-nal

meno mosso.

shower, Or the kiss - es of the sun, Or the dew when day is

done! As she an - - swers yes or no, Darling, take . . . my an - swer

so . . . As she an - swers yes or no, . . Darling, take . . . my answer so.

THE LOVER AND THE BIRD.

P. D. GUGLIELMO.

1. Oh! sing, sing on, sweet-ly to cheer me, Bird thy mu - sic
2. Oh! sing, sing on, e'en to de - ceive me, Bird with vi - sions

sol-ace will bring, Thou wilt not fly, Why shouldst thou fear me?
glitt'-ring and vain, Vain flatt' - ring hopes; Oh! do not leave me.

Sing of love, of love on - ly sing; Those hon - ied notes of thine,
Sing of love, of love on - ly sing; Soon from my dreams shall I

Thro' me are thrill - ing, This heart, long de - sponding, with pleas - ure fill - ing,
Wa - ken to sor - row, To - day give me rap-ture, I'll weep to - mor - row,

Oh! sing, sing on, sweet - ly to cheer me, Sing of love, of
Oh! sing, sing on, e'en to de - ceive me,

love on - ly sing, Sing, Sing,

Ah! Ah! Ah! Ah!

Ah! ah! ah! Ah! songster pi - ty me, Why can I nev - - er

sing a song of rap - ture like thee?

thee?

O SWALLOW, HAPPY SWALLOW.

Two Part Song.

F. KUCKEN.

Allegretto.

scherz.

1. Sing welcome to the swal - low, He news of summer brings, A - cross the sea, a -
2. Ye lit - tle play - ful lamb - kins, Ye here can safe - ly stay; Ye fear no harm, with

3. Fare - well then to the swal - low, He skims a - long the plain, The home he leaves, be-

far comes he With sunshine on his wings.
fleece so warm, From Winter's bit - ter day.
neath the eaves He soon will seek a - gain.

But when the leaves are fall - ing, No long - er
But when the leaves are fall - ing, And na - ked
But fast the leaves are fall - ing, He can - not

But when the leaves are fall - ing, No long - er will he stay.
But when the leaves are fall - ing, And na - ked is the spray,
But fast the leaves are fall - ing, He can - not lin - ger here.

will he stay.
is the spray.
lin - ger here.

He flies a -
The swallow
When sweet birds

He flies a - ghast from Win - ter's blast, Far, far a -
The swal - low flies to bright - er skies, Far far a -
When sweet birds sing in ear - ly spring, A - gain he

ghast from Winter's blast, He flies a - ghast.
flies To brighter skies, Far, far, a - way.
sing, in ear - ly spring, He will ap - pear.

way, Far, far............. a - way,
way, Far, far............. a - way,
will, He will .... ap - pear,

From Winter's blast, He flies a - ghast, from Winter's blast he a - way, Far, far a -
The swal-low flies to brighter skies, The swallow flies to brighter skies, Far, far a -
When sweet birds sing in ear - ly spring, When sweet birds sing in ear - ly spring, He will ap -

he flies a - way, far, far a - way, far,
far, far a - way, far, far a - way, far,
he will ap - pear, he will ap - pear, He
way, From win - ter's blast, He flies a - ghast, from win - ter's
way. The swal - low flies To bright-er skies the swal-low
pear, He will ap - pear, When sweet birds sing in ear - ly
Ped
sf dim.
a - way, From Win - ter's blast He
a - way, To bright - er skies He
will ap - pear, He will ap - pear, He
blast He flies a - ghast, far, far a - way. From Win-ter's blast He
flies to bright-er skies, Far, far, a - way. To bright-er skies He
spring, a - gain, a - gain he will ap - pear. He will ap - pear, He
legato.
p Ped dim. Ped
dim.
flies a - ghast, Far, far a - way.
flies a - way, Far, far a - way.
will a - pear, In ear - ly spring.
8va
pp Ped pp dim.

'TIS NOT TRUE.

Translated and adapted by **THEODORE T. BARKER.**

Composed by **TITO MATTEI.**

Is't not true? When be - side thee I re -

clined, And dis - coursed to thee of love, Dost thou still re - call to

mind All our throb - bing hearts did prove?

When be - side thee I reclined,

And dis - coursed to thee of love, Ah!

no, 'tis not true! Ah! no, No, 'tis not true! no, no.

Dost thou still re - call to mind,

All........... our beating hearts then..................................... .... did prove?

No 'tis not true! Ah! Dost re - mem - ber? thou did'st say, I will

love thee thro' life as now? But 'twas false - hood thee did swity, From the heart ne'er came the vow!

Dost re - mem - ber, thou did'st say?

Thee I'll love thro' life as now? Ah!

No, 'tis not true! Ah! no, No, 'tis not true! no, no.

Ah! 'twas false - hood thee did sway...... ......

'Twas........... not the heart that spoke................................... the vow.

No, 'tis not true! No, no, not true!............ ......

THE SWALLOW.

The Words from "THE AFTERGLOW."   The Music by CIRO PINSUTI.

1. Ev' - ry po - et sing - - eth, Sweetest strain he knows . .
2. Ris - ing, float - ing, wheel - ing, Thro' the a - zure blaze, . .
3. Thee the suff - erer ly - - ing, Nev - er more to rise, . .

To the bird that bring - - eth Back the sum - mer rose; His
Like a sum - mer feel - - ing Flash'd from o - - ther days;
Bless - es in thy fly - - ing With his fad - ing eyes;

heart's bell he ring - eth, His best song he sing - eth, To the bird that
Old de - lights re - veal - ing, Present sor - rows heal - ing, Flow - ery hopes re -
Tho' his heart be dy - ing. Soft - er in its sigh - ing, As he sees thee

cres.   *f*   *dim.*   *p*

bring - eth Back the sum - mer rose............................
veal - ing, Bloom of bright - er days ....
fly - ing, Near - er Par - a - dise! ....

dim.   *dolce.*

cres.

mf con espress.

Swal - low, swal - low, wel - come Swal - low, Veer - ing
       2. Cir - cling
       3. Bless - ing

8va.

pp sotto voce.

o - ver holt, o - ver holt, and hol - low, Swal - low, swal - low,
ev' - ry holt, ev' - ry holt,

tr

pp

cres.
rit.
wel - come swal - low, Veer - ing o - ver holt . . and
2. Circ - ing ev' - ry
3. Bless - ing
leggiero.
rit. col canto.
1st & 2d times.
a tempo.
hol - - - - low.
p
p
a tempo.
leggiero.
p
p last time.
hol - - - - - - - low!
p
pp

FLY FORTH, O GENTLE DOVE.

SONG.

Poetry by F. E. WEATHERLY, B. A.

Music by CIRO PINSUTI.

Andante grazioso.

1. I sent a let-ter to my love, Made
2. And when beneath her bow'r thou art, And

bright with lov-ing words and sweet,   I gave it to a ten-der dove, To
seest her lean-ing from a-bove,   Fly up-ward straight in-to her heart, And

rall.   *con grazia.*

car-ry to my darling's feet,   Fly forth, O gentle dove, I
nes-tle in the warmth thereof.   My love will love thee for my

un poco rall.   *a tempo.*

cried,   Spread westward, spread thy pinions fleet,   O'er hills, and woods and meadows wide,   And
sake,   And give thee welcome, hap-py dove!   Then westward swift thy journey take,   And

cres.   *rall.*   *cres.*   *dim.*

bear my let-ter to my   sweet!..........   to   my
bear my let-ter to my   love!..........   to   my

cres.   *a tempo.*

rall.

f   *con anima.*   *rall.*   *1*

sweet!   Fly forth, O gentle dove, I cried,   And bear my let-ter to   my sweet!
love!   Then westward swift thy journey take,   And bear my let-ter to   my love!

f   *segua il canto.*   *dim e rall.*   *col canto.*   *a tempo.*

molto. rall.   *2,*

bear my let-ter to   my sweet!
bear my let-ter to   my love!

col canto.   *leggiero brillante.*   *p*

MAID OF ATHENS.

Words by LORD BYRON.

Music by HENRY R. ALLEN.

Andante con molto espressione.

1. Maid of Athens, ere we part, . . . Give, oh, give me back my heart! . . .
3. Maid of Athens, I am gone; . . Think of me, sweet, when a - lone, ...

Or since that has left my breast, . . Keep it now, and take the rest! . . . .
Tho' I fly to Is - tam-bol, . . . A - thens holds my heart and soul, ...

piu lento.
con tenerezza.
Hear my vow, be-fore I go, Hear my vow, be - fore I go, My life, ... I love thee, My
Can I cease to love thee ? no ? Can I cease to love thee ? no ! My life, ... I love thee, My
col canto.
pp
rall.
p a tempo.
f Ped. * Ped. * Ped. * Ped *
dear - est life, I love thee, Hear my vow, before I go, My
dear - est life, I love thee, Can I cease to love thee ? no ! My
secondo la voce al fine.
sf
sf
life, ... I love but thee.
Fine.
a tempo.
mf cres. - - - - - dim. p
Ending for 3d verse.
2d verse.
pp
sf
2. By those tresses un - con-fin'd, . . . Wooed by each Æ - ge - an wind, ...

By those lids whose jet-ty fringe, . . . Kiss thy soft cheeks' blooming tinge, ...
Can I cease to love thee? no! . . . Can I cease to love thee? no! . . . . .

piu lento.

By those wild eyes like the roe, Hear my vow, be-fore I go, My
Can I cease to love thee? no! Hear my vow, be-fore I go, My

brillante.

con tenerezza.

life, ... I love thee, My dear-est life, I love thee,

p a tempo.

D.C. al 𝒮.

Hear my vow, before I go, My life, . . . I love but thee.

secondo la voce al fine.

a tempo.

BREAK, BREAK AT THE FOOT OF THY CRAGS, O SEA.

Poetry by TENNYSON.

Music by F. BOOTT.

nev - er come back to me, . . Will nev - er come back to me.
thoughts that a - rise in me, . . The thoughts that a-rise in me.
Fine.
piu mosso.
Oh well for the fish - er - man's boy, That he shouts with his sis - ter at
mf
play! O well for the sai - lor lad, That he sings in his boat on the

bay! And the state - ly ships go on, To their ha - ven un - der the

hill; . . . But . . . O for the touch of a van - - ish'd hand, And the

rall. — — — — — *a tempo.* *sf* *p*

sound of a voice that is still! But O for the touch of a

cres.

van - - ish'd hand, And the sound of a voice that is still!

Dal Segno.

rall. — — — — — *tempo primo.*

ff *p dim.* *p*

SING, SWEET BIRD.

Written by L. M. THORNTON.

Composed by WILHELM GANZ.

Moderato.

1. Sing, sweet bird, and chase my sorrow, Let me lis-ten to thy strain; From thy warblings
2. Morn and noon and dew-y e - ven, Anxiously for thee I'll wait; Come thou cho-ri-

I can bor - row That which bids me hope again. Let me lis - Hover still around his dwelling,
- ster of heav - en, Cheer a soul dis - con - so-late. So shall time fond thoughts awaken,

There is pleasure where thou art; While thy tale of love thou'rt telling, Say—who can be sad at heart,
Joy once more shall live and reign, And the harp so long for - sa - ken, Yield its dul - cet notes a - gain,

While thy tale of love thou'rt telling, Say who can be sad at heart? Sing, sweet bird, Sing, sweet bird, Let me lis-ten

to thy strain; Sing, sweet bird, Sing, sweet bird, Let me lis-ten to thy strain. Ah! · · sing, sweet

bird, Ah! · · sing, sweet bird, · · · · · · · · · · sing, sweet bird, Ah!

. . sing, sweet bird, Ah!. . . sing, sweet bird, Ah! . . . sing, sweet bird, Ah! sing, Ah! sing, sweet bird.

Sing, sweet bird, Sing, sweet bird, Let me lis - ten,

let me lis - ten to thy strain, Ah! . . . . . to thy

strain. Ah! · · sing, sweet bird, Ah! · · sing, sweet bird, · · · · · · ·

· · · · sing, sweet bird, Ah! · · · · sing, sweet bird, Ah! · · · · sing, sweet

bird, Ah! · · · · sing, sweet bird, Ah! sing, Ah! sing, sweet bird.

WEARY.

Words by FLORENCE L. CARTER.

Music by VIRGINIA GABRIEL.

Andante non troppo.

1. Wea - ry of liv - ing, so wea - ry,   Longing to lie down and die,............ To
2. Wea - ry, so wea - ry of wait-ing,   Waiting for sym-pa - thy sweet,............ For
3. Ti - red, so ti - red of drifting,   A-down the dark stream of life,............

find for the sad heart and dreary,   The end of the pil-grim-age nigh............
something to love, and to love me,   And pleasures that are not so fleet............ For a
Ti - red of breasting the billows,   The billows of toil and of strife............

Wea-ry, so wea-ry of wish-ing,   For a form that has gone from my sight,..... ...... For a
hand to be laid on my fore-head,   A glimpse of the golden brown hair,............ For a
Wishing and waiting so sad-ly,   For love that was sweetest and best,............

voice that is hush'd to me ev-er,   For eyes that to me were so
step that to me was sweet mu-sic,   And a brow that was no-ble and
Will-ing to die, oh! so glad-ly,   If that would bring qui-et and

bright.
fair.
rest.

1 & 2.   3.

I AM CONTENT.

Poetry by CLARIBEL.

Music by C. H. SAINTON.

Andantino. *Andante ad lib.*

I am content, I am content,

Tempo 1o.

I am content to be dwelling in shadow, If on - ly the sun-light may sweep o-ver thee;
I am content if the shadow fall o'er me, If rain - bow of promise shine clear - er for thee;

I am content, tho' the thorns be around me, If on - ly the ro - ses be show-er'd on thee.
I am content, tho' the cas-ket be empty, If on - ly the jew - el have fall - en on thee.

I am content, tho' the northwind be cruel, If sweet southern breezes be comforting thee;
I am content with the des - o-late valley, If on - ly the songbirds are sing-ing to thee;

I am content to a - bide in the darkness, If on - ly the starlight shine brighter for thee.
I am content to drink drops of enjoy - ment, If on - ly the fountain fall freely for thee.

Tempo Io.

I am content to be dwelling in shadow, If only the sunlight may sweep over thee ; I am content, tho' the

thorns be around me, If on - ly the ros - es be shower'd on thee.

I LOVE MY LOVE.

Words by **CH. MACKAY.**　　　　　　　　　　Music by **CIRO PINSUTI.**

Allegretto moderato.

Moderato.

1. What is the meaning of the song.　　That
2. What is the meaning of thy thought,　　O
3. O happy words! at beauty's feet,　　We

rings so clear and loud?　　　　　Thou night-in - gale a - mid the copse,　　Thou
maid - en fair and young?　　　　There is such pleas-ure in thine eyes,　　Such
sing them ere our prime.　　　　And when the ear - ly sum-mer pass,　　And

lark a-bove the cloud? Thou lark a-bove the cloud? What says thy song, thou
mu-sic on thy tongue; Such mu-sic on thy tongue; There is such glo-ry
care comes on with time, And care comes on with time. Still be it ours, in

joy-ous thrush, Up in the wal-nut tree? What says thy song, thou joyous thrush, Up
on thy face, What can the meaning be? There is such glo-ry on thy face, What
Care's despite. To join in cho-rus free, Still be it ours, in Care's despite, To

in the wal-nut tree? What says thy song? What says thy song?....
can the meaning be? O maid-en fair! O maid-en fair!
join in cho-rus free, The hap-py words! The hap-py words!

-gretto moderato.
dim.
p
f
"I love my love, I
love my love, because I know my love loves me," I love my love, I love my love, because I know my love loves me."
rall.
1st & 2d.
col canto.
f a tempo.
3d.
me."
a tempo.
sf

BRIDE BELLS.

Words by FRED. E. WEATHERBY. B. A. Music by JOSEPH L. ROECKEL.

Allegretto.

1. Maid
3. A

mf marcato.

El - sie roams by lane and lea, Her heart beats low and sad, Her tho'ts are far a-
year by seas, A year by lands, A year since then has died. And El - sie at the

way at sea, With her bon - nie sai - lor lad, With her bon - nie sai - lor lad. But
al - tar stands, Her sai - lor at her side, Her sai - lor at her side, While

Kling, lang, ling, She seems to hear her bride bells ring, Kling, lang, ling,
Kling, lang, ling, Their bon-nie bride bells gai - ly ring, Kling, lang, ling,

Marcato.

Kling, lang, ling, . . . She seems to hear her bride bells ring, her
Kling, lang, ling, . . . Their bon - nie bride bells gai - ly ring, their

pp una corda. *tre corda.* *cres.*

Fine.

bride bells ring! 2. That

marcato.

piu lento.

night her lov - er's good ship rode The fu - rious Bis - cay

mf
piu lento.

foam, And as the stream - ing deck he trod, He

thought of her at home, He thought of her at

espressivo.

molto rit.

molto rit colla parte.

home; While Kling, lang, ling, He seem'd to hear his home bells ring! *Kling lang,*

dim. *p* *tempo 1mo.*

mf

dim.

p *p tempo 1mo.* *mf*

ling, Kling, lang, ling, . . He seem'd to hear his home bells ring, his home bells ring!

pp *f*

pp una corda. *tre corde.* *f*

LOOKING BACK.

Words by LOUISA GRAY.

Music by ARTHUR S. SULLIVAN.

1. I heard a voice long years a - go, A voice so wondrous sweet and low, That
2. But ere our sum - mer pass'd a - way, That gen-tle voice was hush'd for aye, I

trembling tears un - bid-den rose From the depths of love's re - pose,............ It
watch'd my love's last smile, and knew, How well the angels lov'd her too,......... Then

float - ed thro' my dreams at night. And made the darkest day seem bright, It
si - lent but with blind-ing tears, I gathered all the love of years, And

rall.

whisper'd to my heart, "My love,"
And nestling there, forgot to rove.
laid it with my dream of old,
Where all I lov'd slept white and cold.

Un poco più lento e con molto tenerezza.

O my love I lov'd her so, My love that lov'd me years a - go, O............ my............

love,.......... .... O........... my love, O my love I loved her so, My

tres largement.

love........... ...... that lov'd me years a - go.

LITTLE MAID OF ARCADEE.

Words by W. S. GILBERT.

Music by ARTHUR S. SULLIVAN.

rall.

Happy little maiden, she, Happy maid of Ar-ca-dee! Happy maid of Ar - ca-dee!

rall.   *colla voce.*   *cres.*   *mf*

Moments sped as moments will, Rap-id - ly e - nough; un-til

f

Af - ter, say, a month or two, Rob-in did as Rob - ins do. Fickle as the month of

p

May, Jilted her and ran a - way! Wretched lit-tle maiden, she! Doleful maid of Arcadee!

rall. e dim.

Doleful maid of Ar - ca - dee! To her lit-tle home she crept, There she sat her down and wept,

Maid-en wept as maidens will, Grew so thin and pale and ill, Till an - oth-er came to woo,

Then again the roses grew; Happy lit-tle maiden, she! Happy maid of Ar - ca - dee!

Happy lit-tle maiden, she! Happy maid of Arcadee! Happy maid of Arca-dee!

SING, BIRDIE SING.

Words by ZEILA.

Music by WILHELM GANZ.

1. Sing, birdie sing, and let thy song   Be of this earth so
2. Sing, birdie sing, where the moun-tains glow,   With blushes to meet day's

bright, so.. bright;   Sing bir - die, sing ...... thy notes pro - long,........ Till
king, day's king.   Sing bir - die, sing where the wa - ters flow,........ And

dim. poco rall.

day glides in - to night, Till day glides in - to night.
murm'ring praises ring, And murm'ring praises ring.

Be

a tempo.

p *poco rall.*

bir - die thy lays in sweet na - ture's praise,.... Sing, bir-die

p *sfz* *acce -*

le - - - ran - do. *ritard.*

sing, sing, birdie sing, sing, bir - die sing,.................................... bir - die

sfz *sfz* *p ritard.*

a tempo.
f *p*

sing, sing.......... sing,........ sing.................bir - die sing, sing,............. sing,............ sing......
a tempo.

f *p*

.... bir-die sing, sing,..... ...... sing, ... sing,................ ....birdie sing,

Sing bir-die sing, till time's no more, Sing un - til thy

poco meno mosso.

little life ends; Thou nev - er canst give to na - ture's store, Meet

rall.

praise for the gifts, for the gifts she sends.

Be

a tempo.

rall.

>*acce* - -

bir - die thy lays in sweet na - - ture's praise,.... Sing, bir-die

sfz

or

sing,........ sing.... bir - die,

la - - *ran* - *do.*

sing, sing birdie sing, sing bir - die, sing,...... .... bir - die

ritard.

sfz

sfz

p

sing. sing.............. sing,............ sing ....bird - die sing, sing,.....

.... sing, ... sing,................ bir - die sing, sing, ... sing,...... ... sing, ...

.... birdie sing.

ROSE-MARIE.

F. E. WEATHERLEY.

J. L. MOLLOY.

O - ver the hills and far a - way, In a village by the sea, A small sweet rose of a maid-en dwells Who is dear, so dear to me, With lov - ing lips and true gray eyes, I call her my Rose - Ma - rie.

O - ver the hills and far a - way, dwells my love, my Rose - Marie.

Moderato.

O - ver the hills and far a - way, Fly bonny bird, fly to the sea,

Blow soft and kind, O west - ern wind, Speak to my love, my love of me, O west - ern wind, O happy bird, Speak! speak to my love of me.

O - ver the hills and far a - way, Fly bonny bird to Rose - Ma-rie.

pp

O - ver the hills and far a - way,

To the vil - lage by the sea, I come to bring my

bride from the west, To bring home my sweet to me, O

leave thy home be - side the foam, Come, come sweet

love to me...... O - ver the hills and far a - way,

Come to me, come my Rose - - Ma - rie.

colla voce.   *pp*   *ppp*

SWEET AND LOW.

Written by ALFRED TENNYSON.

Composed by J. BARNBY.

SOPRANO: 1. Sweet and low, Sweet and low, Wind of the wes - tern sea,

TENOR: 2. Sleep and rest, sleep and rest, Fa - ther will come to thee soon.

Low, low, breathe and blow, Wind of the wes - tern sea. O - ver the roll - ing

O - - ver the
Fa - - ther will

Rest, rest, on mother's breast, Fa - ther will come to thee soon. Fa - ther will come to his

wa - ters go. Come from the dy - ing moon and blow, Blow him a - gain to

wa - ters go. Come from the moon and blow,
come to his babe. Sil - ver sails, all out of the west,

babe in the nest. Sil - ver sails all out of the west, Un - der the sil - ver

wa - ters go. Come from the moon and blow, Blow him a - gain to
babe in the nest. Sil - ver sails out of the west, Un - der the sil - ver

me, While my lit - tle one, while my pret - ty one, sleeps.

moon. Sleep, my lit - tle one, sleep, my pret - ty one, sleep.

me.
moon.

THE BELLS OF ABERDOVEY.

"WELSH MELODY."

Eng. words by WALTER MAYNARD.

Accomp. by BRINLEY RICHARDS.

1. In the peace - ful ev'n - ing time, Oft I lis - - ten to the chime;
2. When at morn I used to hear, O'er the hills, their voi - ces clear;

To the dul - cet, ring - ing rhyme, Of the bells of A - ber - do - vey, One, two, three, four,
They would then my young heart cheer, Those sweet bells of A - ber - do - vey, One, two, three, four,

Hark! they ring! Ah! long-lost thoughts to me they bring, Those sweet bells of A - ber - do - vey,
they did sound, And then the e - choes would re-sound, To the bells of A - ber - do - vey,

I first heard them years a - go, When care - less and light-heart - ed,
All their mu - sic seem'd to me, Full of loud mirth and pleas - ure,

I thought not of com - ing woe, Nor of bright days de - part - ed,
And I sung right mer - ri - ly, To its me - lo - dious mea - sure,

Now those hours are past and gone, "When the strife of life is done, Peace is found in Heav'n a-lone," Say the

bells of A - ber - do - vey.

SING, SMILE, SLEEP!

Poetry by VICTOR HUGO.

Music by CH. GOUNOD.

Arranged by S. BEHRENS.

1. When thy voice 'neath the moon's bright beams   I   do   hear,..... ......
2. The   smile   on thy lips gives love's gleam,   to   thine eye,............
3. As   calm   in mine   arms   thou   dost   re - pose,........

'Tis   my   soul's.......... deepest tho't that in   me - lo - dy, mel - o - dy flows,.....................
Prom-ise   of............ bliss and truth in both   age   and   youth,........................
Oft   mur - - mur'd in dreams my name........ I   do   hear...................

Joy smiles as in youth, fad - ed hope, fad - ed hope a - gain grows,..........
And my melt - ing heart pre - pares for the sky,............
On thy beauties I gaze, press thy lips, thy lips of rose,............

.... Ah!.............................. ....
.... Ah!....
.... Ah!....

then sing, then sing my
then smile, oh smile my
oh sleep, oh sleep my

love, my love, sing till the stars ap - pear, then sing,.....................
love, my love, oh smile thy smile of truth, then smile,...... ....
love, oh sleep, oh sleep, sleep with - out fear, oh sleep.. ....

My love, my love 'till the stars ap - pear. Oh sing my..........
My love oh smile thy smile of truth, Oh smile my..........
My love oh sleep, oh sleep my love, Oh

love 'till stars ap - pear................. ....
love thy smile of truth...

last time.

sleep my love oh sleep, sleep with - out

fear....... ....

PALM-BRANCHES.

Translated and adapted by
THEODORE T. BARKER.

Music by J. FAURE.

Andante maestoso.

1. O'er all the way, green palms and blos - - soms gay,
2. His word goes forth, and peo - ple by its might,
3. Sing and re - joice, oh blest Je - - ru - - sa - - lem.

For 2d Verse.

Are strewn this day in fes - tal pre - - pa - ra - - tion,
Once more re - gain freedom from de - - gra - da - - tion,
Of all thy sons sing the e - man - - ci - pa - - tion,

Where Je - sus comes, to wipe our tears a - - way.
Hu - man - i - ty doth give to each his right.
Through bound - less love, the Christ of Beth - le - hem.

rall.

E'en now the throng to wel - come him pre - pare ;
While those in dark - ness find re - stored the light,
Brings faith and hope to thee for - ev - - er - more,

cres. *ff* *Slargando.*

a tempo.

Join all and sing His name, de - clare,

mf

Let eve - ry voice re - sound with ac - - cla - ma - - tion, Ho -

p *cres.* *f*

san - - na! praised be the Lord!

slargando. Largo.

Bless Him, who cometh to bring us sal - va -

tion! . .

1st & 2d. last time.

NAZARETH.

Words by HENRY F. CHORLEY.

Music by CHARLES GOUNOD.

Moderato quasi Andante.

Though poor be the cham - ber, come here, come and a - dore; ....

Lo! the Lord of Hea - - ven Hath to mor - tals giv - - en

Life for e - ver-more, Life for e - ver-more, ...

Life for e - ver - more. . . . . .

Shep - herds, who fold - - ed your flocks be - side you, Tell what was

told by an - - gel voices near: . . . To you this night . . . is

born, He who will guide you Thro' paths of peace to

liv ing wa - ters clear. . . . Though poor be the cham - ber, come here, come and a-

colla voce.

dore, . . . Lo! the Lord of Hea - ven Hath to mor - tals giv - en

Life for e ver - more. . . . . .

Kings from a far land, draw near and be - hold Him, Led by the beam whose warn-ing bade ye come, ... Your crowns cast down, ... with

robe roy-al en-fold Him; Your King de-scends to

earth from bright-er home. ... Though poor be the cham-ber, come here, come and a-

-dore, ... Lo! the Lord of Hea-ven Hath to mor-tals giv-en

Life for e - ver - more. . . . .

Wind to the ce - dars pro - claim the joy - ful sto - ry,

Wave of the sea, . . . the ti - - dings bear a - far, . . . The

night is gone! . . Be - hold, in all its glo - - ry, All

cres.

cres - - - *cen* - - *do.* - -

Ped. ✻ *Ped.* ✻ *Ped.* ✻ *Ped.* ✻ *Ped.* ✻ *Ped.* ✻ *Ped.* ✻

broad and bright ri - ses th' E-ter - - nal morn - ing Star. . . .

Though poor be the cham - ber, come here, come and a - dore; . . . .

Lo! the Lord of Hea - - ven Hath to mor - tals giv - - en

Life for e - ver-more, Life for e - vermore, . . Life for e - ver-more.

THOUGHT CANNOT REACH THEE.

MOZART.

Thought can-not reach thee, Fan - cy not dream; Love! what can

teach thee, Bright, ho - ly theme? Love! what can

teach thee, Bright, ho - ly theme? Blos - - soms are

ly - ing,   Pil - lowed in   bliss,   Zeph - yr a   sigh - ing,

Steal - eth to   kiss ;   While   they were   sleep - ing,   Night   too had

woo'd,   For   with her   weep - ing   They   are be - dew'd ;

Night   soon hath van - ished,   Zeph - yr is   hush'd ;   Dew,   be thou ban - ish'd, Morn - ing hath blush'd! Light yields their bloom - ing,

El - o - quent love, Grate - ful per - fum - ing, Breathes they ap -

prove. Thus, should Affection With early fears, Sigh its se-lection In trembling tears; Cast off the

sadness, Woo by a smile! Earth's every glad - ness, Then shall be - guile.

Sought I to teach thee, Ma - gi - cal theme? Love! nought can

reach thee, Save thy own dream, Love! nought can

reach thee, Save thy own dream, Love! nought can

reach thee, Save thine own dream.

ESMERALDA.

Written by **ANDREW HALLIDAY**, Esq.   Composed by **W. C. LEVEY.**

Tempo di Bolero.

1. Where   is   the lit - tle Gip-sy's home?   Un - der the spreading greenwood tree,   Wher-
2. O   leave her like the bird to   sing,   To sing   on ev' - ry tree and bow'r,   Oh

o - ver she may roam,   Where - e'er   that tree may   be.
leave   her like the bee,   To flit   from flow'r to   flow'r.

Roaming the wide world o'er, Cross - - ing the deep blue sea, She finds on ev' - ry

shore, A home a-mong the free, She finds on ev' - ry

shore, A home a-mong the free, Ah! . . . . Voi -

la La Gi - ta - na, Voi - la La Gi - ta - na, Es - me-ral - da,

Es - me-ral - da, Es - me-ral - da, Zin - ga - ra, Voi - la, La Gi -

ta - na, Voi - la, La Gi - ta - na, Es - me-ral - da, Es - me-ral - da,

Es - me-ral - da, Zin - ga - ra.

The Gip - sy is like the bird, A bird that sings in tree and bow'r, The

Gip - sy is like the bee, The bee that flits from flow'r to flow'r. . . . She

loves the sun and sky, . . . She loves the song and dance, . . . The

groves of sun - ny Spain, The plains of La Belle France, La Belle France.

leggiero.
La Voi - la, Gi - ta - na, La Zin - ga - ra,
Ped * Ped * Ped * Ped *
La Voi - la, Gi - ta - na, Zin - ga - ra.
p f p
Ped * Ped *
2
ra, Oui, Voi-la, La Zin - ga - ra,
ff ff 8va
Ped * Ped *
difficile. grande.
Ah . . . . . Ah . . Voi-la, . . .
facile.
Ah . . . . Voila, La Zin - ga - ra. . . .
8va
ff ff ff ff
Ped * Ped * Ped * Ped *

THE BALLAD SINGER.

(WAKING AT EARLY DAY.)

LINLEY.

1. Waking at ear-ly day,........ Gai-ly I take my way, Trilling some ancient lay,
2. Humble tho' be my fare, Health is a boon I share; Lit - tle I dream of care,

As I stroll a - long, Youthful hearts I cheer, Age delights to hear,
As thro' life I go, None my steps mo - lest, If fatigued, op - pressed,

Gay and grave draw near,.... While I sing my song.
'Neath some tree I rest.........And there for-get my woe.

Far...... I've been........ ...... on dis - - tant strand, Where Chris - tian war - riors
All .... some kind - - ness show to me, Where e'er I chance to

fell; .... Ma - - ny a tale .... of ho - - ly
roam, ... Though...... a wand' - - ring life......... ... I

rall. ———— *tempo.*

land To gen - - tle dames........ I tell,......... .... Waking at ear-ly
lead, I al - - ways find......... a home,......... .... Waking at ear-ly

day, ... Gai - ly I take my way,......... Trilling some an - cient lay,.........

As I stroll a - long, Youthful hearts I cheer, Age delights to hear,

rall. *tempo.* *più mosso.*

Gay and grave draw near,.... While I sing my song,...... .. Tra............ la la

la,........... la la la la la la la la la............ Tra ....la la la............ la la

rall.

la la la la la la la............

TENDER AND TRUE, ADIEU!

GASTON LYLE.

stole from its nest in my gold - en hair, A knot of rib - bon blue, He placed on my hand a jew - el rare, And whis - pered soft as he

held it there, Ten - - der and true, A -

dieu! a - dieu! Ten - - der and

true, A - dieu! a - dieu! a - dieu!

Affettuoso.

almond was bending with blos-soms white, The roses still blushed with the dew;
brought my sol - dier home to me, And my knot of rib - bon blue,

cres. *dim.* *con espressione.*

vi - o - let smiled in the glow - ing light, And life was hap-py and hope seem'd bright;
cru - el wound on his brow was hid By the flag draped over the cof - fin lid;

Ten - - der and true, A - dieu!........... A - dieu!...........

Ten - - der and true, *Appassionato.* A - dieu!........ a - dieu!..... .. a -

dieu!

p

f Stringendo, *Dim.* *Rall.* *tr*

BEAUTIFUL BIRD, SING ON.

T. H. HOWE.

1. Beautiful bird,   in the morning sing,   Messenger dear, . . the sunlight to bring, . . .
2. Beautiful bird,   in the window sing,   Melo- - dies rare, . . bright herald of spring, . . .
3. Welcome the morn - ing smile on the hill;   Sing o - pen the eyes, . . . then slumbering still, ...

While there are sor - rowing hearts to cheer,   Beautiful bird, ... thy mission is clear . . . .
Little bird ren - der for summers to come,   Happy the heart, . . . and happy the home. . . . .
And when the sha - dows of evening fall,   Sing a good night   to the lit-tle ones all. . . . .

Fly while the morning dew sil - vers thy wing, Bright with the lus - tre of ear - ly spring.
Sing at the parting to soft - en the pain, Sing till the greeting brings joy a - gain,
Sing to the ma - ri - ner out on the sea, Sing of the home he is longing to see,

Singing wherever the dark shadows fall, One lit-tle song will dis - pel them all. . . . .
Ev - er keep flying near sorrow and pain, Sing back the smile to the sad eyes a - gain. . . . Sing
When loved ones vanish, and bright hopes decay ; Sing in the wil - low shade so ten - der - ly. . . .

on, ... Sing on, ... Beau-ti - ful, beau - ti - ful bird, ... Sing on, . . . Sing on . . . Beautiful bird, sing . .

on, sing on. . . . .

AULD ROBIN GRAY.

RECITATIVE.

When the sheep are in the fauld, And a' the kye at

hame, And all the weary warld asleep is gone; The waes o' my

heart fall in showers frae my ee, While my gude man sleeps sound by me.

LENTO.

Young Ja-mie lo'ed me weel, and sought me for his bride; But sav - ing a crown, he had
My fa-ther could na work, my mith - er could na spin; I toiled day and night, but their

naething else be - side. To make the crown a pound, my Ja - mie gaed to sea, And the
bread I could na win; Auld Rob maintained them baith, and wi' tears in his e'e, Said,

crown and the pound, they were baith for me. He hadna been a - wa' a
"Jennie, for their sakes will you mar - ry me?" My heart it said nae, and I

week, but on - ly twa, When my mith - er she fell sick, and the cow was stow'n a-wa'; My
looked for Ja - mie back; But hard .. blew the winds, and his ship .. was a wrack; His

father brak' his arm,   my Ja-mie at   the sea,   And auld Rob - in Gray came a
ship it was a wrack!   why did - na Jen - nie die?   And wherefore was I spared to cry,

court - ing me.
" Wae is me!"

3

My father argued sair; my mither didna speak,
But she looked in my face till my heart was like to break
They gied him my hand, but my heart was in the sea;
And so auld Robin Gray he was gudeman to me.
I hadna been his wife a week but only four,
When, mournfu' as I sat on the stane at the door,
I saw my Jamie's ghaist, I couldna think it he,
Till he said, "I'm come hame, my love, to marry thee!"

4

O, sair, sair did we greet, and mickle did we say,
Ae kiss we took—na mair—I bade him gang awa.'
I wish that I were dead; but I'm na like to dee,
And why do I live to say, " Wae is me ?"
I gang like a ghaist, and I carena to spin,
I darena think of Jamie, for that would be a sin;
But I will do my best a gudewife aye to be,
For auld Robin Gray he is kind to me.

ANGELS EVER BRIGHT AND FAIR.

From THEODORA.   *HANDEL.*

Recitative.

O, worse than Death in-deed! lead me, ye guards, Lead me, or to the rack, or to the flames, I'll thank your gra-cious mer-cy.

Piano.

An - gels, ev - er bright and fair,

An - gels, ev - er bright and fair, Take, O take me,   Take, O take me to your

care, ... Take me,   Take, O take me,   An - gels ev - er bright and fair, Take, O take me to your care;

Take, O, take me to your care!

rall: *mf tempo.*

Speed to your own courts my flight, Clad in robes of vir - gin

p *cres - - - - - - - - - -*

white; Clad in robes of vir - gin white, Clad in robes of vir - gin white; Take me,

p

An - gels, ev - er bright and fair, Take, O take me, Take, O take me to your

care, ... Take me, Take, O take me, An - gels

ev - er bright and fair, Take, O take me to your care;

Take, O, take me to your care! *tempo.*

"YOU AND I."

Words and Music by CLARIBEL

1. We sat   by   the riv - er, you and
2. 'Tis years   since we part-ed, you and

I,   In   the sweet summer time, long a - go . . . . .   So
I,   In that sweet summer time, long a - go . . . . .   And I

smooth - ly the wa - ter glided by, Making mu-sic in its tran - quil
smile as I pass the riv - er by, And I gaze in - to the shadow depths be-

flow; We threw two leaf-lets, you and I, To the
low: I look on the grass and bending reeds, And I

riv - er, as it wan - der'd on, And one was rent and left to
lis - ten to the sooth - ing song, And I en - vy the calm and hap-py

die, And the other floated forward all a - lone, And
life Of the riv - er as it sings and flows a - long, For

oh! we were sadden'd, you and I,   For we felt that our youth's gold-en
oh! how its song brings back to me,   The shade of our youth's gold-en

dream   Might   fade, and our lives be sever'd soon,   As the
dream,   In the days ere we part-ed, you and I,   As the

two leaves were parted   in the stream . . . . .
two leaves were parted   on the stream . . . . .

THE DAY IS DONE.

Words by LONGFELLOW.

Music by M. W. BALFE.

The day is done and the dark - ness

Falls from the wings of night; As a feath - er is waft - ed downward From an

Ea - gle in his flight, From an Ea - gle in his flight.

I see the lights of the vil - lage, Gleam through the rain and the mist, And a feel - ing of sad - ness comes o'er me, That my soul cannot re - sist; A feel - ing of sad - ness and longing, That is not a - kin to pain, And re - sembles sor - row on - ly As the mist re - sem - - - bles rain.　　　　　　　　Come read to me some

poem, some sim - ple and heart - felt lay; That shall soothe this rest - less

feeling, And ban - ish the thoughts of day.　　Not from the grand old

mas - ters, Not from the bards sub-lime, Whose dis - tant foot - steps e - - - cho through the cor - - ri - dors of time. For like

accelerando. *cres.*

strains of mar - - tial mu - sic, Their migh - - - ty thoughts sug -

string. *cres.*

gest Life's end - - less toil and en - deav - or, And to -

f rall. *riten.*

night I long for rest, To - night I long for rest.

Tempo 1mo.   *sotto voce.*

Read from some hum-bler poet, Whose songs gush'd

dolce.

from his heart, from his heart; As showers from the clouds of sum-mer, or

tears from the eye-lids start, Or tears from the eye-lids start.

dim. Who thro' long days of la-bor, And nights de-void of

animando un poco. pp

cres.
case, Still heard in his soul the mu - sic Of won - derful mel - - o -
cres.
poco meno mosso.
dies. Such songs have pow - er to qui - et The rest - less pulse of
pp staccato.
Solemnly and slow.
smorz.
care, And come like the ben - e - dic - tion, That fol - lows af - - - - ter
pp colla parte.
cres.
riten.
prayer. Then read from the treasur'd volume, The po - em of thy choice, And
pp riten.

lend to the rhyme of the po - et, The beau - ty of thy voice. And the

night shall be fill'd with mu - sic, And the cares that in- fest the day, Shall

fold their tents like the Arabs, And as si - lent-ly, si - lent-ly,

And as si - - lent - ly steal a - - - - way.

O FAIR DOVE! O FOND DOVE!

Words by JEAN INGELOW.　　　　　　　Music by ALFRED SCOTT GATTY.

Allegro moderato.

rall. — *p a tempo*

1. Me-thought the stars were
2. My true love fares on

blink - ing bright, And the old brig's sails un - furled: I said "I will sail to my
this great hill, Feed - ing his sheep for aye: I look'd in his hut, but

love this night, At the oth-er side of the world"— I stepp'd a - board, we
all was still, My love was gone a - - way, I went to gaze in the

cres.

sail'd so fast— The sun shot up from the bourne; But a dove that perch'd up -
for - est creek, And the dove mourn'd on a - pace, No flame did flash, nor

cres. — *mf*

poco lento con molto espress.

on the mast, Did mourn, and mourn, and mourn. O fair dove! O fond dove! And
fair blue reek, Rose up to shew me his place. O last love! O first love! My

dim. e rall.

poco lento.

dove with the white, white breast! Let me a-lone, the dream is my own, And my
love with the true, true heart! To think I have come to this your home, And

pp rall.

heart is full of rest.
yet we are a-part.

3. My

pp rall.

mf a tempo.

rall.

mf

cres.

love he stood at my right hand, His eyes were grave and sweet; Me-thought he said In

mf a tempo.

cres.

this fair land, O is it thus we meet! Ah, maid, most dear, I am not here, I

have no place, no part— No dwelling more by sea or shore, But on-ly in thy

heart. O fair dove! O fond dove! 'till night rose o-ver the bourne, The

dove on the mast, as we sail'd fast, Did mourn, and mourn, and mourn. ....

CONSIDER THE LILIES.

Andante.

Is not the life more than meat, and the bo - dy than raiment? Be -

hold! the fowls of the air, for they sow not,

nei - ther do they reap nor ga - - - ther in - to barns; yet your Heavenly Father

feed - - - - - - eth them.

Con - sid - - er the lil - ies of the field, how they grow, they toil not,

p *Ped.*
semplicemente.

nei - ther do they spin, . . . they toil not, nei - ther do they spin, ...

And yet I say un - to you, ... I say un - to you that e - ven

cres.

Solomon in all his glo - ry was not ar - rayed like one . . . . of

f *dim.* *p*

these.... Con - sid - - er the lil-ies how they grow,.... Con - sid - - er the

lil-ies how they grow,..... they toil not, they toil not,

nei - - ther do they spin, yet I say un - - to

you, Sol-omon in all his glo - - - ry

154

was not ar - rayed, was not ar - rayed like one of these.........

.... was not ar - rayed,

was not ar - rayed

like one of these, and yet I say un - - to you,

Sol-omon in all his glo - - ry was not arrayed, was not arrayed,

was not arrayed like one . . . . . . of these, ... like one of

these, like one . . . . . . of these.

SHE WANDERED DOWN THE MOUNTAIN SIDE.

Arr. for Piano, by T. B.

1. She wander'd down the mountain side, With measur'd tread, with measur'd tread and slow,
2. Poor child! he's gone to his last rest, A - las! he per - ish'd in a for - eign land,

She heard the bell at ev - en - tide, Down in the vale below, the vale be - low; A bird was
He nobly died with face to foe, Slain by a ruthless hand, a ruthless hand; Ah me! she

sing - ing its psalms of rest, But she heed - ed, heed - ed not its
knows not what they mean, For she heeds not ·········· what they

song, For oth - er thoughts fill'd full her breast, And she
say, And still at ev - en - tide a - gain she's seen, And she

un poco piu lento.

sang as she went a - long— I shall meet him where we al - ways
sings, as she wends her way— *Ritard.*

meet, He is wait - - ing, wait - - ing for me, My heart is

full, I hear it beat, I am com - ing, my love to

thee, My heart is full, I can hear it beat, I am com - ing, I am

com - ing, I am com - - - - - - ing oh my love, to thee.

- - - - ing, oh my love, to thee.

NANCY LEE.

Words by FRED. E. WEATHERLY, M.A.

Music by STEPHEN ADAMS.

With Spirit.

1. Of all........ the wives as e'er you know,................ Yeo ho!....... lads, ho! Yeo
2. The har - bor's past, the breez-es blow,................ Yeo ho!........ lads, ho! Yeo
3. The bo' - s'n pipes the watch be - low,..... .... Yeo ho !........ lads, ho! Yeo

ho!........ yeo ho! There's none like Nancy Lee I trow,................... Yeo
ho!........ yeo ho! 'Tis long ere we come back I know,................... Yeo
ho!........ yeo ho! Then here's a health a - fore we go,................... Yeo

ho! .. lads, ho! .... yeo   ho!
ho! .... lads, ho! .... yeo   ho!
ho!   lads, ho! .... yeo   ho!

See there   she stands an' waves her hands, up-
But true   an' bright from morn till night, my
A long,   long life   to   my sweet wife, and

on .... the quay,   An' ev' - ry day   when I'm   a - way, She'll watch .... for
home ...... will be,   An' all   so neat, an' snug, an' sweet, for Jack ...... at
mates ...... at   sea ;   An' keep our bones from Da - vy Jones, wher-e'er .... we

me,   An' whis - per low,   when tem-pests blow,   for Jack ...... at sea,   Yeo
sea,   An' Nan - cy's face   to bless the place,   an' wel - - come me,   Yo'
be,   An' may   you meet   a mate as sweet   as Nan - - cy Lee,   Ye-

5
rall.
a tempo.
ho!.... lads, ho! ... yeo ho! The sai - lor's wife, the sailor's star shall be, Yeo
rall
p
ho!... ..... we go a - cross the sea,...... The sai - lor's wife, the sailor's star.... shall
f
1 & 2.
be, The sailor's wife, his star shall be............
voce.
f
ff
3
star shall be............
ff
colla voce.
ff

THOU EVERYWHERE.

ÜBERALL DU.

J. LACHNER.

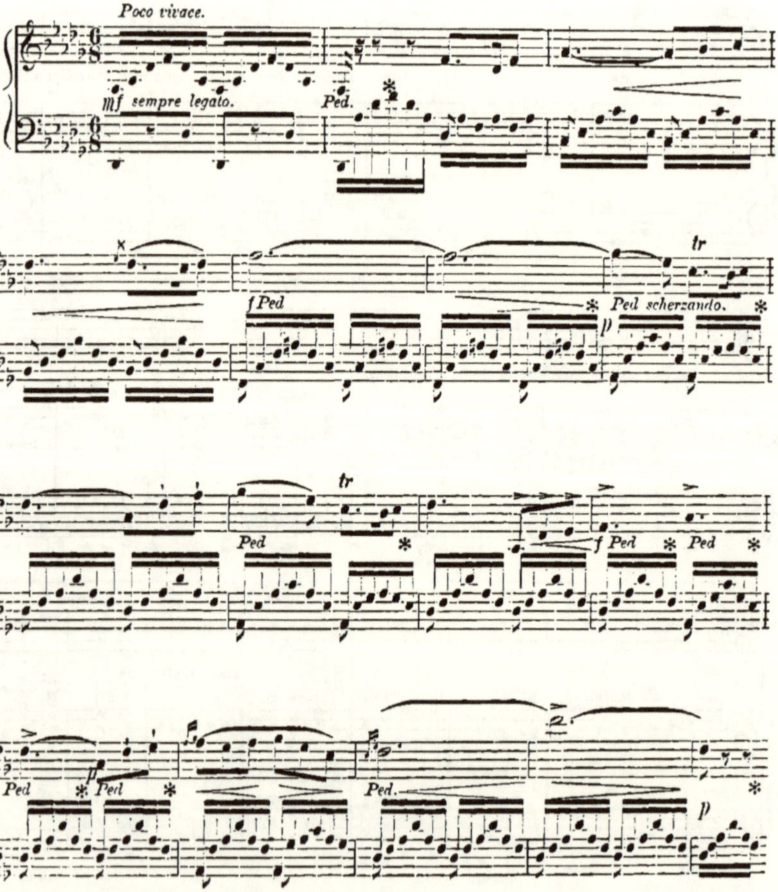

J. Lachner.

1. O'er me night's gloo · · · · my veil; Waiting the day-dawn pale, I count the hours.
1. Wenn mich der dunk · · · · te Schacht Schau-ri - ger Mit - ternacht ein - sam um - schliesst,
2. Then in the lark's......... clear song, I hear; Thy name at eve lulls me to rest.
2. Weckst mich im Ler · · · · chen - sang, und dei - nes Namens Klang, lull't mich zur Ruh.

Watching for morning pale, I count the hours. Yet all is
Schau-ri - ger Mit - ternacht ein - sam um - schliesst, Bin - - ich doch
At eve thy name lulls me to tran - quil rest. Ah! ev' - ry
Und d i - nes Na - mens Klang, lull't mich zur Ruh! Ach! je - nes

bright to me. Love, while I think of thee. As when the shad - ows flee;
me al - lein, denk, ja, Ge - lieb - te, dein, die mir der Lie - - be Pein
pic - ture fair. Doth thy dear im - age bear, Thou dost my soul il - lume,
süs - se Bild, das mir so hell und mild, Leuch - - tend die we - - le füllt,

Morn gilds the bow'rs, Love fills my heart with bliss, sun - - shine, and
Schmerz - lich ver - süsst, die mir der Lie - be Pein Schmerz - - lich ver -
O, maid most dear, Thou dost my soul il - lume, Maid ev - er
Theu - - re bist Du! Leuch - - tend die Ste - - le füllt, Theu - - re bist

1st. time.
flow'rs.
- süsst;
(2nd. time omit.)
mf
f
Ped.
When morn - ing shines on me, Then thy dear form I see,
Du blickst im Mor - gen - schein, bricht dann der A - bend ein,
p
In all things fair, ... In all things fair, In day's ef -
Wink'st du mir zu, ... Wink'st du mir zu. Du in des
8va
- ful - gent glow, In brooklet's tran - quil flow, In star - light, tem - pest, thou
Ta - - ges Gluth, Du in des Ba - ches Fluth, Du in der Stür - me Wuth,

art ev'-ry-where, Nought do I view but thee, thee, ev'-ry-
ä - - - ber - all Du! .Du in der Stür- - me Wuth, ä - - - - ber - - all

- where. dear. Oh! maid .... ev - er
Du! Du! O Theu - - re bist

dear! Oh! maid ... ... ev - er
Du! O Theu ... re bist

dear!
Du!

HUNTING TOWER.

John Demar.

JAMIE. 2. I'll send ye a braw new gown, Jea - nie, the braw - est in the town, las - sie; And

JEANIE. 1. When ye gang a - wa, Ja - mie, Far a - cross the sea, lad - die;

it shall be o' silk and gowd, Wi' Va - len - ciennes set round, las - sie.

When ye gang to Ger - ma - nie, What will ye send to me, lad - die?

JEANIE 3 That's nae gift ava, Jamie,
  Silk and gowd and a', laddie,
  There's ne'er a gown in a' the land
  I'd like, when ye're awa, laddie.

5 Be my gudeman yoursel, Jamie,
  Marry me yoursel, laddie,
  And tak' me ower to Germanie,
  Wi' you at hame to dwell, laddie.

7 Ye shou'd hae telt me that in time, Jamie,
  Ye shou'd hae telt me that lang syne, laddie,
  For had I kent o'your fause heart,
  You ne'er had gotten mine, laddie.

9 Gae back to your wife and hame, Jamie,
  Gae back to your bairnies three, laddie;
  And I will pray they ne'er may thole
  A broken heart like me, laddie.

11 Think weel for fear ye rue, Jamie,
  Ye'll no get ane mair true, laddie,
  But I have neither gowd nor lands,
  To be a match for you, laddie.

JAMIE. 4 When I come back again, Jeanie,
  Frae a foreign land, lassie,
  I'll bring wi' me a Gallant gay,
  To be your ain gude man, lassie.

6 I dinna ken how that wad do, Jeanie,
  I dinna see how that can be, lassie,
  For I've a wife and bairnies three,
  And I'm no sure how ye'd agree, lassie.

8 Your een like a spell, Jeanie,
  Mair sweet than I could tell, lassie,
  That ilka day bewitch'd me sae,
  I could na help mysel, lassie.

10 Dry that tearfu ee, Jeanie,
  Grieve na mair for me, lassie,
  I've neither wife, nor bairnies three,
  And I'll wed nane but thee, lassie.

12 Blair in Athol's mine, Jeanie,
  Fair Dunkeld is mine, lassie,
  Saint Johnstoun's bow'r, and Hunting tow'r;
  And a' that's mine is thine, lassie.

"WHO'S AT MY WINDOW?"

Written by H. B. FARNIE.

Composed by G. A. OSBORNE.

Who's at my window? At . . break of day, Min - strel or lov - er,

Say, . . . oh, say? Sweet through my dreaming Com - eth a strain,

rall.

Who is the sing - er? Dream I in vain!

FLUTE.

rall. f p

mf Lively.

Oh ! 'tis the sky-lark

Soar - ing on high, Bear - ing a mes - sage From earth to the

sky: Trill on ! trill on ! O bird of dawn,

8va

FLUTE.

FAG.

Thy ca-rol gay, Fore tells the day, Ah! Ah!

Ah!

Who's at my win-dow,

When day doth fail? Thou art the minstrel, Sweet nightingale. sweet night-in-gale. Some-thing of sad - ness Lurks ... in thy

song .... Night on thee a - las! Its shade will pro - long! Trill

on! Trill on! Tho' the day is gone, Thy song is light Un - to the night.

Who's at my win - dow At break of day? Min - strel or

lov-er, Say ... oh say! Sweet through my dreaming

Com-eth a strain, Who is the sing-er? Dream I in vain!

p Anime. La la la la .... la la la la .... 'Tis the sky-lark Mounting on high,

Ah! ....

"KILLARNEY."

M. W. BALFE.

Moderato

1 By   Killar - ney's lakes and fells,   Em' - rald isles and wind-ing bays,
2. In - - nis-fal - len's   ruined   shrine,   May   suggest a   pass-ing sigh.
3. No   place else can charm the eye   With   such bright and va - ried tints,
4. Mu - - sic there for e - cho dwells,   Makes   each sound a   har - mo - ny,

Moun - tain paths and woodland dells,   Mem' - ry ev - - er fond - ly strays.
But   man's faith can ne'er de - cline,   Such   God's won - ders float - ing by.
Ev' - - ry rock that you pass by,   Ver - - dure broi - ders or   besprints,
Ma - - ny voiced the cho - rus swells,   'Till   it faints in ex - - ta-cy.

Boun - teous na - ture loves all lands, Beau - ty wan - ders
Cas - - tle Lough and Gle - na Bay, Moun - - tains Tore and
Vir - - gin there the green grass grows, Ev' - - ry morn springs
With the charm-ful tints be - low, Seems the heav'n a -

cres. *rf pp*

ev' - ry where, Foot - prints leaves on ma - ny strands, But her home is
Ea - gle's nest, Still at Mu - cross you must pray, Though the monks are
na - tal day, Bright hued ber - ries daff the snows, Smil - - ing win - ter's
bove to vie, All rich col - ors that we know, Tinge the cloud wreaths

rall. *colla parte.*

dim. *pp a tempo.*

sure - ly there! An - gels fold their wings and rest, In that E - den
now at rest. An - gels won - der not that man There would fain pro -
frown a - way. An - gels oft - en paus - ing there, Doubt if E - den
in that sky. Wings of An - gels so might shine, Glanc - ing back soft

riten. *pp a tempo.*

of the west, Beau - ty's home Kil - - lar - - ney, Ev er fair Kil-
long life's span, Beau - ty's home Kil - - lar - - ney, Ev er fair Kil-
were more fair, Beau - ty's home Kil - - lar - - ney, Ev er fair Kil-
light di - vine, Beau - ty's home Kil - - lar - - ney, Ev - er fair Kil-

lar - ney.

RUBY.

Words by J. J. LONSDALE.

Music by VIRGINIA GABRIEL.

1. o - pened the leaves of a book last night, The dust on its cov - er lay
2. more I was watching her deep fringed eyes, Bent o - ver the Tas - so up -

dusk and brown, As I held - it to-ward the wan - ing light, A
on her knee, And the fair face blushing with sweet sur - prise At the

mf

with - ered floweret fell rus - tling down; 'Twas on - ly the wraith of a
pas - sion - ate pleading that broke from me! Oh Ru - by! my dar - ling, the

cres.

wood - land weed, Which a dear dead hand in the days of old, Had
small white hand, Which gathered the hare - bell was nev - er my own, But

cres.

accel.

placed twixt the pa - ges she loved to read, At the time when my vows of
fa - ded and passed to the far off land, And I dreamt by the flick'r - ing

f ———— *pp*   *con molto espress.*

allargando.   *a tempo.*

love were told, And mem - o - ries sweet but as sad as sweet, Swift
flame a - lone, I gath - ered the flower and I closed the leaves, And

allargando.   *pp a tempo*

flooded mine eyes with re - gret - - ful tears, When the dry dim hare - bell
folded my hands in si - - lent prayer, That the reap - er death as he

skimm'd past my feet, Re - call - ing an hour from the van - ish - ed years.
seeks his sheaves, Might hast - en the hour of our

meet - - ing there, of our

piu lento.

meet - ing there, of our meet - ing there.

SPEAK TO ME!

Written by H. B. FARNIE.

Music by FABIO CAMPANA.

Sostenuto assai.

con espress.

rall.

p a tempo.

Cantabile espress e molto accentato.

1. Why turn a - way,　When I draw near?　Why cold to-day?　Once I was dear!
2. One i - dle day　Thou didst de-plore　Some cast a - way　On de - sert shore;

rall.

Then, thy heart stirr'd,　And flush'd thy brow,　Never a word　Welcomes me now.
'Twas but a tale　By po - et feigned,　Yet thou didst pale,　Si - lent and pained,

rall col canto.

a tempo.

Now thy hand lies　List-less in mine,　Once its re - plies　Spake love di-
And thou didst moan;　Sad, sad to be　Ut - ter - ly lone　By the bleak

sf

vine!............ Cold as if we Nev-er had met, Can it then be
sea!............ My life is drear, I cast a-way, Give me the tear

rall. *a tempo.* *a tempo.*

Hearts can for-get? Ah!............ Speak, to me, speak, Be my heart
Thou shedd'st that day!

col canto. *col canto.* *a tempo.*

con grazia.

heard, Or will it break, For one poor word! No vow to bind,

con grazia.
rall. 1 2

No pledge I seek, On-ly be kind, Speak, to me, speak! speak!

rall. col canto.

JUDITH.

SCENE AND AIR.

French Words by MR. BELANGER.

Music by J. CONCONE.

Translated and adapted by T. T. BARKER.

Allegro.

Recit.

Beneath the ramparts of Bé - thu - la Ho-lopher-nes hath marshalled his in - fa - mous
Sous les remparts de Bé - thu - li - e Holopherne a con - duit ses in - fa - mes sol -

hosts. He hath de - vo - ted us to their im - pi - ous
dats. Il nous a dé - vou - és à sa fu - reur im -

Allegro.

fu - ry, And tomorrow the sun shall look down for my country, But will find it no more.
pi - o; et demain le so - leil cherche - ra ma pa - tri - e qu'il ne re - ver - ra pas.

Moderato.

Our God . . a - lone can save . . us From foes that would en -
Pour no - - tre de - li - vran - - ce Dieu seul en sa puis -

slave us, His arm . . can aid af - ford, His arm can aid afford: A -
san - ce pour - rait, ... combattre en - cor, pour - rait combattre en - cor: he -

dol.

las! . . . . a God un - bend - ing, In wrath at our of - fend - ing, De -
las, ... un Dieu se - vè - - re, nous livre en sa co - lè - - re, au

votes us to the sword, . . Devotes us to the sword.
glai - ve de la mort, ... Au glai - ve de la mort. . . . .

♩ 50.

Cantabile espressivo.

Largemente.

Look down and pi-ty our con-di - - tion, Grant us thine aid in our sub-mis - - sion,
Ah! prends pi-tié de nos a - lar - - mes, de tes en-fants be-nis les ar - - mes,

Thou see'st O God, our deep con-tri - tion, Our hea-vy woes should mer - cy claim.
Dieu, juste et bon, tu vois nos lar - - mes, no-tre mal-heur tu doit flé - chir.

To save our homes from devas-ta - - tion, Life would I give a free ob-la - tion,
Pour le sa-lut de ma Pa-tri - e si je pouvais donner ma vi - e,

And for the er-rors of my na - - tion Proudly I'd march, yes, proudly I'd march to death and
au pied des murs de Be-thu-li - - e je se-rais fie-re, je se-rais fie-re de mon-

a volente.

suivez la voix.

shame! Oh, God, thou see'st our deep con-tri - - - - tion, Our heavy woes should mer-cy
rir! Dieu, juste et bon, tu vois nos lar - - - - mes, no-tre mal-heur te doit flé-

ritard.

claim, Look down and pi-ty our sad con-di-tion, Grant us thine aid in our submission, Thou seest, Oh God, our deep con-
chir! ah! prends pitie de nos a-larmes, de tes enfants be-nis les armes; Dieu, juste et bon, tu vois nos

- tri - tion, Our hea-vy woes should mer - - cy claim, should mer - - - cy claim.
armes,. no - tre mal-heur te doit - - flé-chir, te doit - - - flé-chir!

pp

Allegro moderato.
♩ 112.

Ah! what a rapturous thought inspires with-in my bo-som a pro-ject sub-
Mais, quel transport sou-dain me fait ger-mer dans l'ame un pro-jet glo-ri

a volonté.

lime; Is not the glorious dream a ray of light ce-les-tial, whose blaze illumes mine eyes! . . .
eux! n'est ce pas le ra-yon du-ne ce-les-te flam-me qui vient frapper mes yeux!........

a tempo.

cres. animé.

Allegretto giusto animato.
♩ 112.

cres.

ff

f p

Yes, 'tis God who or-dains me, and to vic-t'ry con-strains . . me,
Oui, c'est Dieu qui m'ap-pel-le, et je mar-che fi-de-le.

'Tis his voice that sus-tains me, that im-pels me a - long, When this sword of sal -
a la voix im - mor-tel - le qui prè - cé - de mes pas! Quand ce fer le - gi -
va - tion strike the foe of our na - tion Fill'd with ho - ly e - la - tion, My
ti - me, frap-pe - ra sa vic - ti - me le de - voir qui m'a - ni - me af -
arm shall then be strong. Yes, 'tis God who or - dains me, And to vic - t'ry con - strains me,
fer - mi - ra mon bras! Oui, c'est Dieu qui m'ap-pel - le, et je mar - che fi - de - le,
Largement a volonte.
and to vic-t'ry con - strains me, that im - pels me, that im - pels me a - long.
a la voix im - mor - tel - le, qui pre - ce - de, qui pre - ce - de mes pas.
avec la voix.
Plus anime.

a volonte.

Is it not God, the Lord, who comes to touch my heart?
N'est ce pas le Seigneur, qui vient toucher mon coeur?

Tempo 1mo.

Yes! 'tis God who or-dains me, and to vic'-t'ry con-strains..... me,
Oui, c'est Dieu qui m'ap-pel-le, et je mar-che fi-dè-le,

'Tis his voice that sus-tains me, that im-pels me a-long, When this sword of sal-
a la voix im-mor-tel-le qui pré-cé-de mes pas! Quand ce fer le gi-

va-tion strikes the foe of our na-tion, Fill'd with ho-ly e-la-tion, my
ti-me, frap-pe-ra sa vic-ti-me, le de-voir qui m'a-ni-me af-

arm shall then be strong. Yes! 'tis God who or-dains me, And to vic - t'ry con - strains me,
fer - mi - ra mon bras. Oui, c'est Dieu qui m'appel - le et je mar - che fi - de - - le,

a volonte. *a tempo.*

'Tis his voice that sus - tains me, That im - pels me, that im - pels me a - long. Ah! yes, 'tis God or-
a la voix im - mor - tel - - le, qui pre - ce - de, qui pre - ce - de mes pas! Oui c'est Dieu qui m'ap -

avec la voix. *trem.*

a volonte.

dains me, to vic - t'ry he con-strains me, His voice from heav'n sus-tains me. And im - pels me a -
pel - le et je mar - che fi - de - le, a la voix im - mor - tel - le, qui pre - ce - - de mes

a tempo.

long. By heav'n's own con - se - ern - - - - tion This sword shall save our na - tion With God's own an - i -
pas! quand ce fer le - gi - ti - me frap - pe - ra sa vic - ti - me le de - voir qui m'a -

trem.

Largement a volonte.

ma - tion My arm shall then be strong, My arm shall then . . . . be strong.
ni - me af - fer - mi - ra mon bras, af - fer - mi - ra . . . . mon bras.

Fine.

ff ff

EMBARRASSMENT.

VERLEGENHEIT.

ALTO SONG.

FRANZ ABT,

Andantino.

con leggierezza.

1. To tell thee something I am yearn - ing, Yet how to speak it, know not
1. Ich möch - te dir wohl et was sa - gen und weiss doch selbst so recht nicht,
2. To thee with joy would I be sing - ing, A song which in my heart is
2. Ich möch - te dir so ger - ne sin - gen ein Lied, das tief in's Herz dir
3. I'd write a let - ter to thee, tell - ing, How deep and hid-den are my
3. Ich möch - te dir ein Brief-lein schrei - ben da - rin mein Herz dir schüt - ten

well; Yet would'st thou still the clue be learning, I on - ly could as answer tell: I
was? und wür - dest du darum mich fra - gen, wüsst' ich wohl sel-ber nichts als das: Ich
heard; But still my lips are only bringing, One soul - felt, tender, pleading word: I
dringt Doch will mir eines nur ge - lin - gen, das stets in mei-ner See - le klingt: Ich
sighs; But from my breast, with passion swelling, One sim - ple word will on - ly rise: I
aus; al - lein auch das muss unter - blei - ben, denn stets bring ich nur das her - aus: Ich

molto espressivo.

love thee dar - ling, faith - ful - ly, Love thee, and on - ly thee,............ I

lie - be dich herz - in - nig-lich, nur dich al - lein, nur dich,........ ich

love thee dar - ling, faith - ful - ly, Love thee,.............. and on - ly

lie - be dich herz - in - nig - lich, nur dich .... al - lein, nur

1 & 2.

thee!

dich!

Tempo 1.

3.

thee!............................

dich!......... ., ...

I LOVE MY LOVE IN THE MORNING.

FOUR - PART SONG.

Words by GERALD GRIFFIN.   Music by GEORGE B. ALLEN.

1. I love my love in the morning, For she like morn is fair, is fair, Her blushing cheek, Its

2. I love my love in the morning, I love my love at noon, at noon, For she is bright as a

3. I love my love in the morning, I love my love at even, at even, Her smile's soft play is

p leggiero.

crim-son streak, Its clouds, her gold-en hair; Her glance, its beams so soft and kind, Her

ray of light, Yet mild as Autumn's moon; Her beau - ty is my bos - om's sun, Her

like the ray That light the western heaven; I lov'd her when the sun was high, I

ad lib. *poco piu lento.* *rall.*

tears, its dew - y show'rs, And her voice, the ten-der whisp'ring wind, That stirs the ear - ly

faith my fost'ring shade. And I will love my dar - ling one, 'Till even the sun shall

lov'd her when he rose, Yes, But best of all when evening's sigh was murm'ring at its

poco piu lento.

sf *rall.*

a tempo. *rall.*

bow'rs. Oh! I love my love in the morn - ing, For she like morn is fair.

rall.

fade. Oh! I love my love in the morn - ing, I love my love at noon.

close. Oh! I love my love in the morn - ing, I love my love at even.

a tempo. *rall.*

f *p* *a tempo.* *rall.*

THE "BRIGHT BEYOND."

T. H. HOWE.

love   the rest re-flec-tion brings   When my heart is sad... and wea - ry,   I
spell   fond mem'ries gently weave   Brings the heart hope bright - ly beam - ing   To

love   to hear the bird that sings   From my soul the sha - dows drear - y,   I
all   who thro' night's sorrow grieve,   Breaks the dawn of morn - ing gleam - ing,   For

love   to listen for the chime   When the sweet bells ring back the "Old - en Time," The
An - gels hov-er far and near,   O'er the green graves whisper they, "not here, not here," Tho'

Lyrics under staves:

tones with mem'ries full and fond | sun - dered ev'-ry earthly bond, | I hear re-echoed in the "Bright Beyond," Then voi - ces softly seem to | There's hope; re - u-nion in the "Bright Beyond,"Fall o'er the grave the shadows

sing, | may, | From my soul the sha - dows drear - y,........ Then comes the rest re - flection | But the beau - ty bright and ver - nal....... Ap - pears from over the si-lent

brings | way | When the heart is sad and wea - ry. | To re -

2. The - flect the Spring E - ter - nal.

FAR AWAY.

Words from
SUMMER SONGS OF COUNTRY LIFE.

Music by
Miss M. LINDSAY.

1. Where is now the mer-ry par-ty, I re-mem-ber long a-go; Laughing round the Christmas fire,....... Brighten'd by its rud-dy glow:

2. Some have gone to lands far dis-tant, And with stran-gers made their home, Some up on the world of wa-ters, All their lives are forced to roam;

3. There are still some few re-main-ing, Who re-mind us of the past, But they change as all things change here, Noth-ing in this world can last,

Or in sum - mer's balm- y eve - nings, In the field up - on the
Some are gone from us for - ev - er, Long - er here they might not
Years roll on, and pass for - ev - er, What is com - ing, who can

un poco cres.

. hay! They have all dis-pers'd and wan - der'd Far a - way, ... far a -
stay— They have reach'd a fair - er re - gion Far a - way, ... far a -
say? Ere this clos - es, ma - ny may be Far a - way .... far a -

dim. *p*

way, They have all dis-pers'd and wan - der'd Far a - way, ... far a -
way, They have reach'd a fair - er re - gion Far a - way, ... far a -
way, Ere this clo - ses, ma - ny may be Far a - way, ... far a -

1st & 2d time. last time.

pp

way. way.

mf *p* *pp*

BY THE BLUE SEA.

Words by FREDERICK ENOCH.

Music by HENRY SMART.

1. I stood where the summer tide, flow - ing, Homeward the bark gai - ly
2. I thought of brave sails homeward wing - ing, Tide waves of mem' - ry

bore.............. But I saw the same O - cean was throw - ing
bore............. To the heart while its wa - ters were fling - ing

To - kens of wreck on the shore. While a voice mid the tide's song of
To - kens of wreck to the shore, And I felt, as o'er mem' - ry

glad - ness,   Sighed   thro' its   sweet - ness   to   me,   And it
near - er   Hopes   freight with   joy   came to   me,   Still the

fill'd   all   my heart with a   sad - ness,   By   the blue . . . .
wreck'd and the bro - ken were   dear - er,   By   the blue . . . . .

sea,   By the blue   sea,   By the blue . . .

. . . . the blue   sea.

OH! HOW DELIGHTFUL.

Words by A. SKETCHLEY.

WALTZ SONG.

Music by J. L. MOLLOY.

1. Oh! how de - light - ful, Oh! how en - tranc - ing,
2. Oft when dark sha - dows are o'er us creep - ing,

From this drear thral - dom soon to be free, With wild - est joy, then,
And check the throb - bing of youth - ful hearts, Hope like a sun - beam

my heart is danc - ing, Dancing so gai - ly now with glee.
watch near us keep - ing, Breaks thro' the gloom and joy im - parts.

From morn till night im - pris - on'd here, Pass'd we our days . . in
No long - er shall we droop and pine, In drea - ry hours . . our

gloom . . and fear; No joys to cheer us, no de - light,
lives . . . a - way, When clouds are dark - est, oft doth shine,

rall.

All . . was drea - - ry, noth - ing bright, Now, how de - light - ful,
Soft - ly and bright - ly, hope's cheering ray. Yes how de - light - ful,

rall.

now, how en - tranc - ing, From this drear thraldom soon to be free,
yes, how en - tranc - ing. From this drear thraldom soon to be free, &c.

With wild-est joy, then, my heart is danc - ing, Danc-ing so gai - - ly now with glee. Ah . . . . Ah . . .

my heart is danc - ing now with glee. Ah . . . . Ah . . .

. . . my heart is danc - ing now . . with glee.

THE BRIDGE.

Words by LONGFELLOW.

Music by LADY CAREW.

stood on the Bridge at midnight, As the clocks were striking the hour, And the moon rose o'er the

ci-ty Behind the dark church tow'r. Among the long black rafters, The

wav'ring shadows lay; And the current that came from the ocean, Seem'd to lift and bear them a-way.

As sweeping, eddying through them, Rose the be-lat-ed tide, And streaming in-to the

moon - light The sea-weed float-ed wide; And like those waters rushing, A-

mong the wooden piers, A flood of thoughts came

o'er me That fill'd my eyes with tears,

How oft - en! O how oft - en   In the days that had gone by,   I had stood on that bridge at

legat:

mid - night, And gaz'd on that wave and sky,   How oft - en! O how oft en,   I had

wish'd that the ebbing   tide,   Would bear me away on its bosom, O'er the o - cean wild and wide.

Agitato.

For my heart was hot and   restless,   And my life   was full   of care;   And the

accel.

ad lib.
p a tempo.

bur - den laid up - on me Seem'd greater than I could bear; But now it has fallen

p

from me, It lies buried in the sea; And on - ly the sor - row of

others, Throws a shadow o - ver me; And I think how ma-ny thousands Of

care - encumber'd men, Each bearing his burden of sorrows, Have cross'd the bridge since then.

For ev-er and for ev-er, As long as the river flows, As long as the heart has

rall.   *a tempo.*

passions, As long as life has woes, The moon and its broken reflection. And its

rall.

shadows shall appear, As the symbol of love in Heaven, And its wav' - ring im - age

here.

CHRISTMAS SONG.

With accompaniment for Reed Organ.

English Words by J. S. DWIGHT, Esq.   Music by ADOLPHE ADAM.

Andante Maestoso.

1. O ho - ly night! the stars are brightly shin - ing; It is the
2. Led by the light of Faith serene-ly beam - ing, With glowing
3. Tru - ly he taught us to love one an - oth - er; His law is

night of the dear Saviour's birth!   Long lay the world in sin and er - ror
hearts by his cra - dle we stand: So, led by light of a star sweetly
Love and his gos - pel is Peace;   Chains shall he break, for the slave is our

pp
pi - ning, 'Till he appeared, and the soul felt its worth, A thrill of hope the
gleam - ing, Here came the wise men from the O - rient land, The King of Kings lay
broth - er, And in his name, all oppres - sion shall cease, Sweet hymns of joy in
pp
weary world rejoic - es, For yon-der breaks a new and glorious morn! Fall.... on your knees. . ..... O
thus in low-ly manger, In all our tri - als born to be our friend; He.... knows our need, ... to our
grateful Chorus raise we; Let all with - in us praise his Ho-ly name! CHRIST is the LORD!.... .. ..
cres.
f

hear.... the an-gel voi - ces! O night.... di - vine!.... O night when CHRIST was
weak - ness no stran - ger! Be-hold...... your KING! .... Be - fore him LOWLY
then ev-er! ev-er praise we! His pow'r.... and glo - ry, ev - ermore pro-

born. O night .... di - vine.... O night, O night di - vine.
bend! Be - hold...... your KING! your KING! be - fore him bend.
claim! His pow'r........ and glo - ry, ev - er-more proclaim!

THE MAIDEN'S ROSE.

Or, SO THE STORY GOES.

Words by Dr. J. F. WALLER.

Music by J. L. HATTON.

Allegro.

f brillante.

1. 'Twas once up - on a sum - mer day,
2. The mil - ler's son stood by the bank,

So the sto - ry goes. The Franklin's daughter chanc'd to stray Where the mill-stream
So the sto - ry goes. He stopp'd the wheel, and ere it sank, Caught up the maid - en's

flows. And as the rus - tic bridge she cross'd, So the sto - ry goes,
rose. "Is this thy flow'r, sweet heart?" he cried, So the sto - ry goes.

ad lib.
Tempo piu animato.
O - ver the rail she stooped, and lost From out her breast a rose. The stream ran fast, the
The maiden blush'd, the maid - en sigh'd, "Oh! give me back my rose," "Two flow'rs" he said, "so
colla voce.
p e leggiero.
stream ran strong, So the sto - ry goes. And on its wa - ters
sweet and fair," So the sto - ry goes. "'Twere
cres.
ad lib.
bore a - long The care-less maiden's rose, The care-less maid - en's rose, The care-less
maid - en's rose.
f
sf

shame to part, one breast should bear Thy-self and this red rose, Thy

self and this red rose." What more the youth and

maid-en said, That summer eve, who knows? But he kept the flow'r and

won the maid, So the sto-ry goes.

THE KING'S HIGHWAY.

SONG.

Words by F. E. WEATHERLY.

Music by J. L. MOLLOY.

(♩ = 66.)

f Ped. * Ped. * Ped. * Ped. * Ped. * Ped. * *ril.*

1. Who rides yonder proud and gay, Spurning the dust on the King's Highway? Lord of thousand a - cres wide, While

poco rit - ar - dan - do. *a tempo.*

I, the beggar must stand aside; Go thy way, let me go mine, I to beg, and thou to dine,

ritard.

Scatter the dust on the King's Highway, But room for the beg - gar, room, I say!

con spirito.

Fair and free, Night and day, Fair and free is the King's Highway, Fair and free, Night and day, —

Fair and free is the King's Highway!

Hug thyself in wealth of state, Emp - ty purse has a care - less gait; Thou must watch thy chest and bags,

None would steal the beggar's rags. Wine for thee, for me a crust, King and beggar they both are dust, And dust to dust will be borne one day, High and low on the King's Highway.

Fair and free, Night and day, Fair and free is the King's Highway, Fair and free, Night and day,

Fair and free is the King's Highway! Dain - ty maid of high degree,

What has the beggar to do with thee? Thy life is morn, And love is May;

poco ritard.

What has the beggar to thee to say? Gen - tle word hast thou for me? Tears are in my

heart for thee; Ah! that thou shouldst fade one day, E'en as I on the great High - way!

Fair and free, Night and day, Fair and free is the King's Highway, Fair and free, Night and day,

Fair and free is the King's, the King's High - way!....................

THE KING'S HIGHWAY 4.

THERE'S NOTHING LIKE A FRESH'NING BREEZE.

For Bass or Alto Voice.

ALBERTO RANDEGGER.

1. Give me a fresh'ning breeze, my boys, A white and swelling sail, A ship that cuts the dashing waves, And
2. foaming waves a - round us dash! The an - gry storm loud roars, 'Tis mu - sic to the sail - or's ear, And

weath - ers ev' - ry gale, What life is like a sea - man's life, So free, so bold, so brave. His
high his cour - age soars: He feels a king of migh - ty pow'r, The el - e - ments his slaves, His

home the o - cean's wide expanse, A co - ral bed his grave, ... Hur - rah! .... hur -
trus - ty ship at his command, Steers on thro' storm and waves, .. Hur - rah! .... hur - rah! .... hur -

Cres.

rah! hur - rah, then, for a seaman's life, For o - cean, ship and wind There's nothing like a fresh'ning breeze, To

f mf

sf

cres.

Ped. *

1st time.

gladden heart and mind.

with energy.

ppp a tempo. stacc.

ff

p ff cres. _ _ _ _

cres. _ _ _ _

2nd. *cres.* *ff*

When gladden,heart and mind; Hur - rah!.... har - rah!...... hur - rah!........ har -

ff

ff stacc.

sf

ff affrettando sino al fine.

rah!............................

fff

affrettando sino al fine.

Ped. *

COLINETTE.

English words by L. C. ELSON.

Music by GIULIO ALARY.

Andantino mosso.

1. Co - li-nette was my love's name,
2. When we played the hours a - way,
3. On this bench one e - ven - tide,
4. Ma - ny tales there are I know,

In a qui - et vil - lage dwelling, And the harvest ripe was swelling, When to her home first I
'Mid the fields with verdure teeming, She with glee and mirth was beaming, And I was glad and
We a fond farewell were saying, Love my in-most soul was swaying, Yet I scarce knew why I
Showing love be - reft and lone-ly, Yet there is but this one on - ly, Which can cause my tears to

came, She a maiden, sim - ple heart - ed, And a youthful student I.
gay; By us Finch and Lin - net dart - ed, Sing-ing of our youthful love,
sighed. Then I from thy side de - part - ed, Said "a - dieu," and hid my pain, "Next
flow; Since she left me wea-ry heart - ed, None could e'er my soul en - chain;

Why did she so ear-ly die?
Twitt'ring in the trees a-bove,
year we shall meet a-gain,
I have nev-er loved a-gain,

Why did she so ear-ly die?
Twitt'ring in the trees a-bove,
Next year we shall meet a-gain,"
I have nev-er loved a-gain,

Oh, poor Co-li-
Oh, poor Co-li-
Oh, poor Co-li-
Poor, lost Co-li-

nette! Now we both are part - - ed.
nette! Now we two are part - - ed.
nette! We for aye are part - - ed.
nette! Since we two were part - - ed.

I AM WEARY WITH ROWING.

Words by W. W. STORY.

Music by F. BOOTT.

1. I am wea-ry with row-ing, with row - ing, Let me drift a-long with the stream. I am wea - ry with row - ing, with row - - ing, Let me lay me down and dream. . . .

2. The stream in its flow-ing, its flow - ing, Shall bear us a-down to the sea; I am wea-ry with row - ing, with row - - ing, I yield me to love and to thee. . . .

I can strug - gle no long - er, no long - - - er;

Here in thy arms let me lie, ... In these arms which are

stronger, are strong - er Than all of this earth, Let me die, Let me die.

THE ROSE OF THE ALPS.

Arranged and adapted to English words

By GEORGE LINLEY.

Allegretto.

1. 'Mong the beauteous flow'rs I live, Hap-py as young heart can be,....
2. When the day-light fades a-way, Pleas'd I turn my steps to home,..

There's not a boon the world could give, Like the charm of rov-ing free:
Yet with the first blush of the day, Here with my flocks a-gain I roam;

Ah!... vain-ly, lov-ers en-treat me, Vow... fond and faith-ful to prove;
Ah!... gai-ly, then I am sing-ing, As... i-dly wand'ring a-long.

I am more blest here con-tent-ed to rove, Far from the sorrows and cares of love. Ah!
E - cho re - peating, the mountains a - mong, Ev' - ry wild note of my Al - pine song. Ah!

Ah!

Ah!

THE VAGABOND.

Words by CHAS. LAMB KENNEY.

Music by JAMES L. MOLLOY.

Home - less, rag - ged and tann'd, Un-der the changeful sky, Who so free in the land, Who so con - tent-ed as I? Ne'er .. need I quake, lest for - tune prove un - kind, . . Ne'er . . . my heart break, that vows have ceased to

bind. Not . . . . e'en a dog . . . . Would I call by friendship's name. . .

Lone - - ly I jog . . . . E'en thi - ther whence I came. . . . . .

Home - less, rag-ged and tann'd, Un-der the changeful sky, Who so free in the land, Who so con-tent-ed as I?

Nurs'd by hun-ger and want, Taught out of na-ture's

page, Bann'd by saint-li-est cant, Scorning hy-poc-ri-sy's wage,

Sing - - ing I plod, By way-ward fan - cy led, . . . Trust - ing in

God, Who the sparrows still hath fed, No! . . . let me die, . . . Ere

be the world's base thrall, Fate . . . I de - fy; . . To - mor - row ne'er re -

- call. . . . Home - less, rag-ged and tann'd, Un - der the change-ful sky, Who so free in the land, Who so con-tent-ed as I?

Once,... ten-der love Watch'd at my side, Now,... from a-

-bove.. Her An - gel's my guide. When heav'n a - bove Asks my last

breath, An - - gel love Smile on the Va-ga-bond's death.

When .. heav'n a - bove Asks ... my last breath, An - gel love,

Smile on the Va-gabond's death, Smile on the Va - ga-bond's death. . . . .

poco accel.

Ah! . . . . . Home - less, rag-ged and tann'd, Un - der the change-ful

cres.

sky, Who so free in the land, Who so con-tent-ed as I? . . . .

'TWAS IN THE SUNNY RHINE-LAND.

Or, THE RHINE MAIDEN.

HENRY SMART.

Allegretto moderato.

1. 'Twas in the sun-ny Rhine - land, When
2. I saw her stand-ing all a-lone, The
3. Up - on her im - age in the stream, Re -

gold-en day was end - ing, And ripe grapes in the vine-land, Were in rud - dy clus-ters
chap-el bells were ring - ing, And mingled with their sol-emn tone I heard her gen-tle
flect-ed midst the rush - es, She gaz - es in a pleasant dream, And smiles, and sighs, and

bend - ing.
sing - ing.
blush - es.

The ru - ined tow - er on the height Was
The riv - er ran be - side her feet, And
She takes the ar - row from her hair, And

glow - ing in the crim - son light, The east - ern sun was lend - ing.
Oh! her voice so low and sweet, To heav'n was up - ward ring - ing.
down up - on her shoulders fair, The gold - en show - er gush - es.

I saw her then, I see her yet, It was the first time that we met, In the
I saw her thus at close of day, I gazed and gazed my heart a - way, In the
I watched her as I stood a - part, That sil - ver ar - row pierced my heart, In the

sun - ny Rhine - land.

SOFTLY, SOFTLY, SOLEMN MEASURE.

(PIANO, PIANO.)

"Der Freischütz."

1. Soft - ly, soft - ly, sol - emn meas - ure, Soar a - - loft to deep - est a - -
1. Pia - no, pia - no, can - ta pia - no, Ti sol - le - va fi - nal Di - -
2. To thee pray - ing, I am kneel - ing, Lord e - ter - nal now ap - peal -
2. Dio cle - - men - te, che pos - sen - te, Reg - ni in cie - lo e - ter - na - - men -

- zure, God a - - dor - ing and im - plor - ing Rise...... to
- o, Deh tu pe - ne - tra tu ec - che - gia,...... Nel - la
- ing, Us to shel - ter from all dan - ger, Send, oh
- te, Da te im - plo - re Dio dio a - do - ro, Pel mio

heav'n - ly spheres my pray - - - er.
an - ta ac - cel - sa reg - - - gia.
send thy hosts of an - - - gels.
ben pa - ce s ri - sto - - - ro.

"THE TAR'S FAREWELL."

Words by F. C. BURNAND

Music by STEPHEN ADAMS.

MODERATO CON ENERGIA.

1. When forced to bid farewell to Loo, Pull a-way, my boys, pull a- way,   I   did not know what I should do, Pull a-
2. But then if false should prove my fair, Pull away, my boys, pull a- way,   I'd burn this lit - tle lock of hair, Pull a-

- way,   pull a - way,   I   left her weeping   on the quay, She said she would be true to me, As we
- way,   pull a - way,   If she be false   and I be free, I'll sail a - gain to the Southern sea,

4

rall.

sail'd a - way to the Southern sea; Pull a - way, my boys, pull a - way,   Pull a - way, pull away, pull a -
Where there are plenty as good as she, Pull a - way, my boys, pull a - way,   Pull a - way, pull away, pull a -

p cantabile.

way....................   For the wind must blow, and the ship must go, And

lov - ing souls must part,   But the ship will tack, and the Tar come back To the

con spirito.

first love of his heart,   For the wind must blow, and the ship must go, And

The Tar's Farewell.   3.

lov - ing souls must part, But the ship will tack, and the Tar come back To the

1st. ad lib.

first love of his heart,.... To the first love of his heart.........

p

f

rall.

2d. ad lib.

first love of his heart.

colla voce,

ff

The Tar's Farewell. 3.

A TWILIGHT FANCY,

or DRESDEN CHINA.

Words by F. E. WEATHERLY.

Music by J. L. MOLLOY.

Andante con moto.

1. In the twi-light as I play, And
as I dream in the flickering gleam, He

fan-cies come and go, And dreamland falls on the old oak walls. From the firelight's fitful glow;
takes her wee sweet hand, And too and fro in a measure slow, They tread a sa-ra-band;

Side by side in the cor-ner wide, Stand a lit-tle lass and lad, And thro' the gloom of my
Still they dance and still they play, 'Till the mu-sic gives a sigh, As danc-ing aye, they

lone-ly room Come their two lit-tle fa-ces glad. Side by side in the cor-ner wide, I
fade a-way And in the sha-dows die. Dim-ness falls on the old oak walls, And

watch their ev' - ry look, She peeps at him 'neath her hat's white brim, As he leans on his lit - tle
lone - li - ness on me, When they are gone, my song, is done, And the mu - sic hushed must

rall.

a tempo.

crook. Hour by hour I watch them there, But they take no heed of me, They
be; Oh, how I loved to watch them there, Tho' they took no heed of me, They were

pp a tempo.

make my dark room bright and fair, The lit - tle He and She, They
on - ly Dres-den Chi - na fair, The lit - tle He and

1.

And She.

2.

pp

JAMIE!

Words and Music by **J. L. MOLLOY.**

1. Ja - mie! Ja - mie! Ja - mie! Ja - mie! do you hear me
2. Ja - mie! Ja - mie! Ah! if he were ne - ver,

call-ing in the gloaming, Calling to you, lad - die, to come home; Long and lone I'm watching, and my heart is
ne-ver more to hear me, Ne-ver to come back to me a - gain. Sure I'm on -ly dreaming, and I know he's

wond'ring Why up-on the hill so late you roam, Ja - mie! Ja - mie! Are you ne - ver com - ing
com - ing, All the same the tears will flow like rain. Ja - mie! Ja - mie! Ah! the fear is on me,

Amphion.

ritard. et rall.

To the little heart that's waiting sad at home. Ja - mie! Ja - mie! Ja - mie!
And my heart is ach - ing with dull pain; Ja - mie! Ja - mie! Ja - mie!

ritard. et rall.

Ped. Ped.

a tempo.

Jamie! Do you hear me calling in the gloam-ing, Call-ing to you, lad - die, call-ing Ja - mie!
Jamie! Do you hear me calling in the gloam-ing, Call-ing to you, lad - die, to come home.

a tempo.

f

p pp

3. Ja - mie! e - cho an - swer,

p f pp pp

Ped. Ped.

Joyously.

And it says he's com - ing, com - ing down the hill - side, Well I know his voice, my bon - nie lad,

Ped. Jamie.

Now I hear him sing-ing to the cat-tle blithe-ly, And the lit-tle sheep-bells tink-ling glad,

Ja-mie! Ja-mie! Ah! the joy is on me, and my heart is go-ing just like mad,

Ja-mie! Ja-mie! Ja-mie! Welcome to you, lad-die,

welcome in the gloam-ing, All my heart is cry-ing welcome Ja-mie!

THE LOST CHORD.

Words by ADELAIDE A. PROCTOR.　　　Music by ARTHUR SULLIVAN.

ANDANTE MODERATO.

Seat - ed one day at the or - gan, I was wea - ry, and ill at ease, And my fin - gers wander'd i - dly O - ver the noi - sy keys; I know not what I was play - ing, Or

4

what I was dreaming then, But I struck one chord of mu - sic, Like the

sound of a great A - men, Like the sound of a great........ A-

- men. It

flood - ed the crim - son twilight, Like the close of an An - gel's Psalm, And it

The Lost Chord. 5.

dim. .... 5 ......

lay on my fe-ver'd spi - rit, With a touch of in - fi - nite calm, It

dim. ....

cres. .... *dim.*

qui -et-ed pain and sor - row, Like love o - ver-com - ing strife; It

cres. .... *dim.*

seem'd the har - mo - nious e - - cho From our dis-cor - dant life, It

p *p tranquillo.*

tranquillo sempre.

link'd all per-plex - ed mean-ings, In-to one per - fect peace, And

The Lost Chord. 5.

trem - bled a - way in - to si - lence, As if it were loth to cease; I have

sought, but I seek it vain - ly, That one lost chord di - vine, Which

came from the soul of the or - gan, And en - ter'd in - to

mine. It may be that Death's bright An - gel, Will

The Lost Chord. 5.

speak in that chord a - gain; It may be that on - ly in Heav'n, I shall
sempre. ff
Ped. ✻ Ped. ✻ Ped. ✻ Ped. ✻ Ped. ✻ Ped. ✻
hear that grand A - men. It may be that death's bright An - gel, will
sf sf
Ped. ✻ Ped. ✻ Ped. ✻
ff ritard. con gran forza.
speak in that chord a - gain, It may be that on - ly in Heav'n, I shall
fff ritard. colla voce con gran forza.
hear that grand A - - men.....................
a tempo. rallentando.
Ped. ✻ Ped. ✻ Ped. ✻ Ped. ✻ Ped. ✻ Ped. ✻

LET ME DREAM AGAIN.

Words by B. C. STEPHENSON.

Music by ARTHUR SULLIVAN.

MEZZO SOPRANO.

ANDANTE ESPRESSIVO.

The sun   is   set - ting and the hour   is   late,   Once more   I
The clock   is   strik - ing in the bel - fry tower,   And warns - us

stand   be-side the wick - et   gate,   The bells   are ringing out   the
of   the ev - er fleet - - ing hour,   But nei - ther heeds the time   which

dy - ing day, The chil - dren singing on their home - ward way, And

on - ward glides, For time may pass a - way, but love a-bides. I

cres.   *dim.*   *p*

he   is   whisp'ring words of sweet   in - tent,   While I,   half

feel   his   kiss - es   on my   fe - - vered brow,   If   we must

rall.   *un poco piulento.* ℗ ℗

doubting,   whis - per a consent.   Is   this   a dream?   then

part,   ah ! why should it be now ?   Is   this   a dream?   then

5

wak - ing would be pain, Oh, do not wake me, let me dream a-

-gain. Is this a dream? then wak - ing would be pain,

cres. *cres.*

Oh! do not wake me, do not wake me, let me dream a-gain.

appassionato ad lib.
con forza.

www.ingramcontent.com/pod-product-compliance
Lightning Source LLC
Chambersburg PA
CBHW020853270326
41928CB00006B/691